WHAT ABOUT
KIDS
MINISTRY

WHAT ABOUT KIDS MINISTRY

PRACTICAL ANSWERS TO
QUESTIONS ABOUT KIDS MINISTRY

EDITED BY BILL EMEOTT

B&H
PUBLISHING GROUP
NASHVILLE, TENNESSEE

978-1-5359-2509-9

Published by B&H Publishing Group
Nashville, Tennessee

Dewey Decimal Classification: 259.22
Subject Heading: CHURCH WORK WITH KIDS /
CHILDREN / MINISTRY

Unless otherwise noted, Scripture quotations are taken
from the Christian Standard Bible® Copyright 2017 by
Holman Bible Publishers. Used by permission.

Also used: King James Version (KJV), public domain.

Cover design by Stephanie Salvatore.
Pattern illustration © shutterstock/venimo.

1 2 3 4 5 6 7 • 22 21 20 19 18

CONTENTS

CONTRIBUTORS

Jeremy Carroll has served in kids ministry for twenty-three years. He is a graduate of Middle Tennessee State University and Southwestern Baptist Theological Seminary. Jeremy is a publishing team leader for LifeWay Kids and teaches Bible study and kids worship at his church.

Rachel Coe has served in kids ministry for forty-two years. She is a graduate of Middle Tennessee State University and is a content editor for LifeWay Kids. Rachel teaches preschoolers at her church.

Jeremy Echols has been serving in kids ministry for twenty-one years. He is a graduate of Louisiana College and Southwestern Baptist Theological Seminary. Jeremy is the manager of LifeWay Kids Camps and Events and teaches second and third grade Bible study at his church.

Bill Emeott has been serving in kids ministry for twenty-eight years. He is a graduate of Mercer University and New Orleans Baptist Theological Seminary. Bill is the lead kids ministry specialist at LifeWay Kids and enjoys teaching preschoolers, second graders, and preteens each week at his church.

Shelly D. Harris has been serving in kids ministry for twenty years. She is a graduate of Murray State University and Southern Baptist Theological Seminary. Shelly is a content editor for LifeWay Kids and is the kids ministry associate at her church.

Landry Holmes has been serving in kids ministry for thirty-eight years. He is a graduate of Howard Payne University and Southwestern Baptist Theological Seminary. Landry is the manager of kids ministry publishing at LifeWay Kids and teaches preschool Bible study and Vacation Bible School at his church.

Karen Jones has been serving in kids ministry for nineteen years. She is a graduate of the University of West Georgia and New Orleans Baptist Theological Seminary and is a content editor for LifeWay Kids. Karen teaches three- and four-year-olds in Bible study each week at her church.

Jeff Land has been serving in kids ministry for seventeen years. He is a graduate of Mississippi College and Southwestern Baptist Theological Seminary. Jeff currently serves as children's pastor at Sugar Creek Baptist Church in Sugar Land, Texas. Prior to moving to Texas, Jeff spent twelve years as a publishing team leader for LifeWay Kids.

Jana Magruder has been serving in kids ministry for twenty-three years. She is a graduate of Baylor University and is the director of LifeWay Kids. Jana teaches preteen girls each week and preschoolers during worship at her church.

Chuck Peters has been serving in kids ministry for twenty-six years. He is a graduate of Columbia International University and is the director of operations for LifeWay Kids. Chuck teaches children in weekly Bible study and children's worship at his church.

Tim Pollard has been serving in kids ministry for twenty-three years. He is a graduate of the University of Georgia and New Orleans Baptist Theological Seminary. Tim is a publishing team leader at LifeWay Kids and teaches kids Bible study and boy's missions education at his church each week.

Debbie Ruth has been serving in kids ministry for twenty-eight years. She is a graduate of Middle Tennessee State University and Southwestern Baptist Theological Seminary. Debbie is a content editor for LifeWay Kids and teaches second graders at her church.

Kayla Stevens has been serving in kids ministry for ten years. She is a graduate of William Carey University and Southeastern Baptist Theological Seminary. Kayla is a content editor for LifeWay Kids and enjoys teaching preschoolers and children at her church.

Bekah Stoneking has been serving in kids ministry for nineteen years. Bekah is a graduate of Columbus State University and Southeastern Baptist Theological Seminary. Bekah is a content editor for LifeWay Kids and teaches preschoolers at her church.

Klista Storts is the preschool content editor for LifeWay's Vacation Bible School resources. Prior to LifeWay, Klista served as preschool minister at churches in Oklahoma and Tennessee. She has a passion for training and equipping leaders to share the gospel with kids and their families.

William Summey has been serving in kids ministry for twenty-five years. He is a graduate of Furman University, Southeastern Baptist Theological Seminary, and Vanderbilt University. William is a publishing team leader for LifeWay Kids and teaches each week at his church.

Melita Thomas has been serving in kids ministry for twenty years. She is a graduate of Campbell University and Dallas Baptist University. Melita serves as Vacation Bible School and kids ministry specialist at LifeWay Kids and teaches kindergarten Bible study, Vacation Bible School, and preteen choir at her church.

Rhonda VanCleave has been serving in kids ministry for forty-four years. She is a graduate of Lincoln Memorial University and is a publishing team leader for LifeWay Kids. Rhonda teaches children's worship each week and Vacation Bible School at her church.

Delanee Williams has been serving in kids ministry for twenty-two years. She is a graduate of Baylor University and Southwestern Baptist Theological Seminary. Delanee serves as kids ministry specialist for LifeWay Kids and teaches preschoolers and children at her church.

INTRODUCTION

I knew God called me to ministry. I knew He had placed a burden in my heart specifically for kids ministry, and I realized that He had gifted me with talents that would help me in the role I'd just been chosen to fill. But the truth was, I didn't know what I was doing. I'd had formal education, for which I'm thankful, but I needed quick answers to the everyday questions, issues, and ministry struggles that I now faced and for which I didn't feel equipped.

I was immediately enrolled into the school of hard knocks and began seeking and reading and studying other ministries I thought could give me direction. I was blessed with ministry leaders in my community who had pity on me, perhaps saw potential, and jumped in to give direction and serve as mentors and friends. The first year wasn't easy. But with my calling secure, my support system in place, and the Holy Spirit empowering me, I made it through.

I've often wished there had been a resource that would have quickly answered my questions. I needed a one-stop resource that I could reference and trust. It is in the hopes of offering that resource to others that we offer this compilation.

I couldn't have been the only minister who needed help and answers, and I'm pretty sure there are still many today who are experiencing the same feelings of inadequacy and need for direction and assurance. So I sat with ministry colleagues and began to seek practical answers to questions relevant to today's kids ministry leaders.

I am thankful for the wealth of knowledge represented on these pages. I'm thankful for the answers compiled in this book by ministry experts with vast and varied backgrounds. I'm thankful for their ministry to children and their families. I'm most thankful to God who loves kids, families, and those of us who are trying hard to honor Him as we minister. To God be the glory! Great things He has done and will do through each of you.

CHAPTER 1

WHERE DO I START?

CRAFTING A PLAN FOR YOUR MINISTRY

Introduction

I like to travel. Work-related trips, short weekend trips, or all-out vacations, I'm in. However, I've learned the hard way that preparation for a trip is just as important as the trip itself. Failure to plan can result in unnecessary stress, cost, and a reduced level of productivity and fun.

You'd never start on a trip without knowing where you were going and what it's going to take to get you there. It's the same with kids ministry. The nuts and bolts of your ministry really do matter. Establishing the *why* gives direction for the *who, what, when, where,* and *how.* Starting with a good foundation and a well-thought-out plan makes all the difference.

This chapter is dedicated to some of the foundational questions about kids ministry. Answering these questions will help you ground your kids ministry and keep you headed in the right direction. Knowing the why will keep you focused and help keep you from veering off in the wrong direction.

So, let's get going on the trip of a lifetime.

What about Ministry Philosophy?

by Jana Magruder

"What about ministry philosophy" is really a section about the *why* in kids ministry. Creating and championing a ministry philosophy is arguably the most important task you can do as a new kids minister. *Philosophy* is a word that gets thrown around quite a bit and can mean different things to different people. For the purpose of this chapter, I'd like to focus on philosophy pointing to the core mission and values you put into place that you can always point back to and say, "Our kids ministry is about this." So, what is *this*?

An easy way to conclude what your philosophy of children's ministry consists of is to think through this construct and ask yourself these questions:

1. *What are the closed-handed, nonnegotiable parts of my ministry?* Take a few minutes to write these down. Think about all the things that you would never let go of, what you fight for and stand upon for the ministry God has given you. For example, it may (hopefully, it does) have something to do with evangelism and discipleship.

2. *What are the open-handed, variable parts of my ministry?* Now, spend some time thinking through these items. There likely will be more of these. Examples might include curriculum choice, timing of Vacation Bible School (VBS), how to divide classes, specific safety procedures, and all the endless decisions about activities, snacks, volunteers, etc.

As you can see, there are many decisions about kids ministry that can be seen through the lens of open and closed hands. When it comes to building a philosophy of ministry, it's important to focus on the nonnegotiable portions. What are the essential values, mission, and purpose of this ministry?

In the book *Kids Ministry that Nourishes*, I unpack three "essential nutrients" that contribute to healthy kids ministry. Just like healthy food nourishes our bodies, a healthy ministry can nourish hearts and souls through Jesus. The three essential nutrients are:

Kingdom expanding,
not ministry building

Heart Transformation,
not behavior modification

Culture Shaping,
not shaped by the culture

A ministry philosophy based on a **Kingdom Expanding** mindset is healthy—as opposed to focusing on building up your own ministry. That may sound counterintuitive. You might wonder, "Am I not supposed to build up my ministry?" The problem occurs when ministry building drives us rather than expanding God's kingdom. For example, I remember during my first year as a kids minister I was determined to host the biggest and best VBS our community had ever seen! There's nothing wrong with wildly important goals focused on outreach. However, my vision was slightly blurred by making it about me and the phenomenal VBS I was going to produce, as opposed to turning the focus to a true Kingdom Expanding strategy.

It's necessary to create a philosophy that not only helps you lead yourself, but is also easy to communicate with fellow ministry colleagues, volunteers, and families. If everyone can get on the same page about being a kids ministry that focuses on expanding God's kingdom, then a lot of ministry can flow from that philosophy.

Once a Kingdom Expanding mind-set is established, you are ready to focus on the kids and families God brings into your ministry. Healthy children's ministry is based on the essential nutrient of being **Heart Transforming**. Those of us in kids ministry are in this because we care about the hearts and souls of children. Heart transformation should drive you, as opposed to behavior modification, which can be like a trap. Oftentimes, those of us who work with kids want to see behavior modification. We want to see good morals and values. But if we lead with that, kids may be getting more from their character education classes at school. We must lead with Jesus because He is the only one who can transform hearts, and He does it through His Word. Therefore, the content that we teach should be rooted in Scripture and focused on Christ. We might be able to alter behavior, but we cannot transform hearts. A ministry philosophy that holds heart transformation with closed hands is one that can lead to much fruit.

As kids go through a Heart Transforming ministry, they will have opportunities to trust Jesus as their Lord and Savior. When they do, it changes everything. A healthy kids ministry will be **Culture Shaping**. We have to teach kids that the Great Commission is for them. We want them to impact the world around them for Jesus and share Him with their friends, classmates, teammates, and neighbors. Build in opportunities for kids to hear, learn, and pray for missionaries both locally and abroad. Help them begin to have a heart for the nations. A culture-shaping ministry will thrive as opposed to kids being shaped by the cultures around them. Ultimately, we want the kids in our ministries now to eventually become the goers and senders across the world, proclaiming the gospel for His glory.

As you can see, a healthy ministry philosophy begins with the *why*. Spend some time praying about what your philosophy will be. You can certainly use the three essential nutrients listed here, or let them inform your own. I encourage you to refer to your ministry philosophy often and be sure your church staff and congregation know that you are leading with these in all that you do. The more you use them, the more they will seep into your culture, impacting the ministry God has given for you to lead . . . for His glory!

What about Developing a Vision?

by Landry Holmes

Wait! Before you read this, make sure you have articulated your philosophy of kids ministry and that you have written it down. Vision builds on philosophy. Next comes mission and values. So, you can't really claim to have a vision unless you first have a ministry philosophy that permeates your being.

Caleb was such a person. His phi-losophy was based on the truth that God is

> Vision builds on philosophy.

all-powerful, sovereign, and good. Caleb believed that God would do what He promised. Since God said to take possession of the land He was giving His people, God would make the conquest possible. With complete faith in God, Caleb then was able to articulate his God-given vision.

The scene was quite chaotic. Twelve spies had just returned from their clandestine mission of scouting out the land God had long-promised His chosen people. The purpose of the spies' report was to prepare the Israelites for what they faced when they marched into Canaan—to determine what they were up against and to see God's goodness. The report was to inform their conquest strategy.

Unfortunately, as people are prone to do, the Israelites miscon-strued God's purpose and viewed the mission of the twelve spies as a fact-gathering quest to help them decide whether or not to enter the Promised Land. However, Caleb "quieted the people in the presence of Moses and said, 'Let's go up now and take possession of the land because we can certainly conquer it!'" (Num. 13:30).

Now that is vision. Caleb believed God (philosophy), and God gave Caleb a vision of life in the Promised Land.

Do you believe God when He says we are to, "Imprint these words of mine on your hearts and minds, bind them as a sign on your hands, and let them be a symbol on your foreheads. Teach them to your children, talking about them when you sit in your house and when you walk along the road, when you lie down and when you get up. Write them on the doorposts of your house and on your city gates, so that as long as the heavens are above the earth, your days and those of your children may be many in the land the LORD swore to give your fathers" (Deut. 11:18–21)? If so, then vision naturally will follow.

Vision starts with philosophy and begins moving us toward practical application in kids ministry. To start, ask yourself these questions:

1. What will toddlers look like spiritually when they become preschoolers? What biblical knowledge will they have? What will be their level of biblical literacy? How will they be living in response to God's Word?

2. What will preschoolers look like spiritually when they enter the elementary ministry? What biblical knowledge will they have? What will be their level of biblical literacy? How will they be living in response to God's Word?

3. What will elementary kids look like spiritually when they enter the student ministry? What biblical knowledge will they have? What will be their level of biblical literacy? How will they be living in response to God's Word?

Paul's prayer for the Christians in Ephesus echoes what a God-honoring kids ministry vision looks like:

> For this reason I kneel before the Father from whom every family in heaven and on earth is named. I pray that he may grant you, according to the riches of his glory, to be strengthened with power in your inner being through his Spirit, and that Christ may dwell in your hearts through faith. I pray that you, being rooted and firmly established in love, may be able to comprehend with all the saints what is the length and width, height and depth of God's love, and to know Christ's love that surpasses knowledge, so that you may be filled with all the fullness of God. (Eph. 3:14–19)

In other words, vision reflects your desire for kids to receive God's gift of salvation through His Son and to become more like Jesus. Two tools exist to aid you in knowing how such a vision manifests itself in kids' lives: Levels of Biblical Learning® and Bible Skills for Kids.

If your vision includes Bible knowledge, then the Levels of Biblical Learning can provide a spiritual blueprint comprised of biblical concepts—truths—that kids need to learn as they grow from infancy to the beginning of the teenage years. The concepts are organized by ten major categories: God, Jesus, Holy Spirit, Bible, Salvation, Creation, Family, People, Church, and Community and World. For example, under the concept of Jesus, these are some truths for kids to learn:

- Younger preschool: Jesus was born.
- Middle preschool: God sent Jesus to earth.
- Older preschooler: God sent Jesus to earth as a real person.
- Younger kids: God sent Jesus to earth in human form.

- Middle kids: God planned for Jesus to be the Savior from the beginning of time.
- Preteens: God planned for Jesus to be the Savior from the beginning of time and sent Jesus to earth at the perfect time.

The idea of biblical literacy may also be part of your vision. So many adults who grew up in church know little to nothing about what the Bible is and how to use it. Bible Skills for Kids covers nineteen Bible skills and concepts that preschoolers and elementary kids can learn as they interact with and learn about the Bible. These Bible skills and concepts reflect Bible skill goals kids can reach by the end of the age range given.[1] Here is an example of how the skill of using Bible reference tools plays out:

- Younger preschool: Sees the Bible used to tell a story. Helps open the Bible.
- Older preschool: Begins to use simple tools for Bible discovery (printed and digital resources). Helps open the Bible to a Bible book.
- Younger kids: Locates all books of the Bible by using the contents page or with teacher guidance. Uses other tools for learning from the Bible, including Bible-learning apps, Bible dictionaries, and maps.
- Older kids: Uses other resources to enrich Bible skills and knowledge (Bible dictionary, commentary concordance, atlas, and digital sources).

Whatever vision God gives you, keep in mind that He will empower you to fulfill that vision. Sometimes you just have to be patient. Caleb had to wait over forty years before his vision came to fruition. One of my favorite passages recounts Caleb's speech at the end of that waiting period:

As you see, the LORD has kept me alive these forty-five years as he promised, since the LORD spoke this word to Moses while Israel was journeying in the wilderness. Here I am today, eighty-five years old. I am still as strong today as I was the day Moses sent me out. My strength for battle and for daily tasks is now as it was then. Now give me this hill country the LORD promised me on that day, because you heard then that the Anakim are there, as well as large fortified cities. Perhaps the LORD will be with me and I will drive them out as the LORD promised. (Josh. 14:10–12)

Once God gives you a vision and you can articulate it clearly, begin sharing that vision with key leaders in your church, starting with the senior pastor. With the senior pastor's blessing, guide kids ministry influencers to own the vision as well. One way to do this is to lead the kids ministry team at your church to develop a mission statement and patiently watch God begin to fulfill His promises.

What about a Mission Statement?

by Landry Holmes

The popularity of mission statements has waxed and waned over the years. I think part of the reason for this is a lack of clarity regarding the importance of a mission statement.

More than twenty years ago, I penned a personal mission statement. The substance of the statement is still relevant today because it reflects God's purpose for me to encourage my family to follow Christ, evangelize people with the gospel, equip people for ministry, and experience life with passion. My personal and professional roles have

changed, but God's calling on my life has not. A mission statement—
whether it be for an individual, a secular corporation, or a church—is
timeless. It can change in wording, but its core usually remains the
same for a long period of time.

Another reason we may sometimes roll our eyes when we hear the
term "mission statement" is that it often is found on business cards and
plaques, but many times not lived out in the day-to-day functions of
the organization. A mission statement born out of a God-given vision,
however, can be a powerful tool. If the philosophy and vision of your
church's kids ministry provides the *why* behind what you do, then the
mission statement gives the marching orders to do kids ministry.
Think of your mission statement as the embodiment of your philosophy and vision and as a rallying cry for the work of kids ministry in
your church.

> "Go, therefore, and
> make disciples of all
> nations, baptizing them
> in the name of the
> Father and of the Son
> and of the Holy Spirit."
> (Matt. 28:19)

The difference between corporate and
church mission statements is that Jesus has
already given the local church its mission:
"Go, therefore, and make disciples of all
nations, baptizing them in the name of
the Father and of the Son and of the Holy
Spirit" (Matt. 28:19). Churches then con-
textualize that mission when they develop
their own statement. One church I know
states its mission in this way: "We exist to
glorify God by leading people to become passionately devoted followers of Jesus Christ."[2]

Once you are ready to develop a mission statement based on your
vision, you may want to follow a path similar to this one:

- Identify and enlist kids ministry influencers in your
  church to serve on a short-term team that will
  develop a mission statement. The team should include

individuals who faithfully serve in kids ministry. Be sure to recruit parents as well as other individuals who understand babies through preteens.

- Spend time individually and together as a team praying and reading Scripture passages about the ministry of Jesus and His church.

- Examine and study the church's mission statement. Consider requesting that the senior pastor spend time with the team to explain the church's vision and mission.

- Begin contextualizing the church mission statement by listing words, phrases, and concepts that reflect the kids ministry vision. Include actual words from the church's mission statement.

- Assign one member of the team to write a draft of the mission statement, based on the previous actions.

- As a team, edit the draft and send to the senior pastor or his designee for further edits and/or approval.

- Complete the final draft with the consensus of the team and route to church leaders, kids ministry leaders and teachers, and parents, as directed by the senior pastor or his designee.

Now that a final mission statement is complete, the difficult work of living, teaching, and implementing it begins. The immediate next step is to articulate your church's kids ministry mission.

What about Values?

by Landry Holmes

If philosophy and vision are the *why* behind your church's kids ministry, and your mission statement is an embodiment of that philosophy and vision, then values answer the *what* of kids ministry. What we value determines whether or not we accomplish our mission. More succinctly, our values state what is most important in our church's kids ministry.

> What we value determines whether or not we accomplish our mission.

For example, if your kids ministry "exists to glorify God by introducing children and families to Jesus and leading them to follow Christ," then you might state your values in this way:

- The Bible is True—We present the Bible's content to kids unaltered and without embellishment, at a level they are able to grasp. (2 Tim. 3:16–17)
- Only Jesus Saves—We give kids opportunities to trust in Jesus. (Acts 4:12)
- Parents Disciple—We equip parents to disciple their children. (Deut. 6:7)
- Kids Matter—We love kids and treat them with respect. (Mark 10:13–16)

Of course, you will want to develop your own kids ministry values, following a plan similar to the one outlined in the section, *What about a Mission Statement?*:

- Guide the mission statement team to develop kids ministry value statements.
- Assign someone to write a draft of values.

- As a team, edit the draft and send to the senior pastor or his designee for further edits and/or approval.
- Complete the final draft with the consensus of the team and route to church leaders, kids ministry leaders and teachers, and parents, as directed by the senior pastor or his designee.
- Equip kids ministry leaders and teachers to implement the values.
- Consider posting the values in an attractive format in the preschool and elementary ministries' hallways.
- Make the values language a natural part of your conversations, meetings, and other forms of communication with parents and kids ministry leaders.

You can articulate your kids ministry philosophy and your vision by stating your mission and values. Are you ready to coast through the rest of your leadership responsibilities? Not quite. Now comes more hard work as you develop a strategy to accomplish the mission of your church's kids ministry.

What about Goals?

by Chuck Peters

"Are we there yet?!?" Anyone who has ever taken kids on a road trip has heard this infamous phrase, typically delivered in a grouchy tone that indicates a lack of enthusiasm for the present location and a lack of patience for the remaining duration to be endured before reaching the much-anticipated destination. This first question is often followed by, *"How much longer?"*

As the adult in the driver's seat, you know how many miles you need to travel, how many hours it will take to get there, what landmarks you'll pass along the way, and at what intersections you need to change roads. The kids in the backseat have none of that perspective. They are along for the ride, but they are not engaged in the details of the trip nor involved in controlling the speed or direction of the vehicle. They are strapped in for however long the ride lasts.

As the driver of your ministry, you are in a similar situation; only this time it is your adult team members, leaders, and volunteers who are along for the ride. The people on your team need to know where you are going in terms of ministry goals, what landmarks you expect to pass along the way, and how long it will take to get there. They need to know why you take the turns you choose and how their contribution fits into the big-picture plan. Sadly, many kids ministry leaders cannot articulate specific answers to questions about their goals because they don't know what the goals are themselves. They are moving with direction and driving with passion and purpose, to be sure, but there is no clearly defined and documented destination. In many cases, vision for a ministry does not extend beyond surviving the present hour or the next service—as if driving in the fog. For others, the goal is far away, and there is no road map explaining how to get there.

Setting and tracking goals in kids ministry are as crucial as using GPS on a road trip. Here are a few tips to get you on the right track:

1. **Begin with the destination in mind.** The first step to navigating with GPS is entering the address of your desired destination. In the case of kids ministry, this might mean describing the spiritual characteristics of kids that you want your ministry to produce when they leave your children's ministry for a middle school or high school program. I encourage you to describe these results in terms of a child's heart condition

and their sensitivity to God's will, God's Word, and God's way for their lives—not their outward behavior. While there should be fruit as evidence of a changed heart, if our ministries merely produce well-behaved children who act the part without true heart transformation, we will have done them more harm than good. Ultimately, we are training up children to be mature Christian adults, not just well-behaved kids.

2. **Write it down and talk it up.** Once you have identified your goal, write it down. Committing your goals to paper (or pixels) is a great way to make sure they are clear, concise, and can be easily communicated. Try to make your mission concise enough so you can print it on your T-shirts and plaster it on your walls. People are drawn to organizations with strong, clear objectives that they can connect with. Sharing the purpose of your kids ministry publicly gives others the opportunity to join you on the journey. It also commits you to carrying it out and provides accountability to stay the course.

3. **Set mile marker goals.** The best way to ensure accomplishment of your great big long-term goal is to set a series of short-term goals to mark the way. I recommend having a whole bunch of them. While you don't need every one of these, there is much merit in segmenting your goals into increasingly smaller chunks to make sure that everything you do supports your stated purpose.

   • Nine-year goal—This is the full duration that a child could be in your ministry, from preschool through sixth grade.

- Three-year goal—This is a typical duration of the scope and sequence of a curriculum and covers large spans of development in a child's life. Babies through kindergarten, first grade through third, and fourth grade through sixth.
- One-year goal—What do you hope to accomplish this calendar year, or within each grade-level that kids are in this year?
- Quarterly goal—What are your emphases this quarter?
- Monthly goal—What is your focus this month?
- Weekly goal—What biblical truth, concept, or principle do you hope to convey this week?
- Hourly goal—Within each week there are multiple ministry hours, including multiple services and mid-week times. Each program hour may serve a unique purpose in discipling kids and each should have its own goals.
- Segment goals—Each hourly time slot may contain multiple subsegments for storytelling, Bible memory, worship, and learning activities. Each of these has its own purpose that your teachers should understand.

4. **Stick with your plan.** Once you have set a goal and identified a strategy, it's important to stick with it. When it comes to accomplishing goals, there's a lot to be said for consistency. Kids ministers often get antsy and feel the need to keep changing curriculum on a yearly, quarterly, monthly, or weekly basis. Kids forums online often have questions asking, "What curriculum are you using this month?" I believe this is a disservice to your ministry. Every

curriculum is written from a different foundational approach, so teaching and changing too frequently does not allow the full plan to be realized as the full scope and sequence are administered. Your long-term goals should include a wise plan for discipling kids in regards to the materials you use. Committing to a curriculum with a three-year chronological scope and sequence would allow you to take a child all the way through the Bible three times from birth to sixth grade before they leave your ministry. If you are not pleased with the content of your current curriculum, by all means, look for something better, but as you evaluate any curriculum, do so with the intention of using it for its full cycle, and choose one that you can commit to for the long haul.

Having clearly defined goals for your ministry will give you wonderful perspective that you can use as a road map to evaluate the activities, resources, and strategies you choose to use or avoid. Communicating your destination will let everyone, from parents to volunteers, know exactly what they are signing up for. Giving your passengers regular updates along the way will help everyone better enjoy the ride.

What about Communicating These Things?

by Chuck Peters

Formulating a philosophy of ministry, crafting vision, mission, and values statements, determining how you will define success within your ministry area, and setting strategic goals are absolutely essential to leading an intentional team toward an efficient and effective kids ministry. Together, all of these things make up the *why* of your kids program. They serve to clarify the direction, purpose, and pace of your ministry. A clearly defined *why* serves as both a target and a filter as you consider actions you might take.

While formulating a compelling *why* for your ministry is an important first step, simply having a *why* is not enough. As the leader of your ministry, you are responsible to not only determine your *why*, but to share it with others in a way that is clear, concise, and compelling. Unless you communicate your purpose in a way that connects with your team, church leadership, and parents, you may as well not have one at all. Here are some tips for communicating your *why* in the best possible way:

> As the leader of your ministry, you are responsible to not only determine your *why*, but to share it with others in a way that is clear, concise, and compelling.

1. **Take it slowly.** Adopting and communicating a new *why* for your ministry can change the entire dynamic of your church culture. While that may be exactly what your church needs, big changes can also be threatening to those who are comfortable with your current culture and to those who are averse to change. It is important that you ease into big changes and give people time to know your heart and to buy into a new vision themselves. This is particularly important if you are new in your role or new to your church. People naturally fear that new leaders will institute unwelcome and unnecessary changes without team input. It's best to take time to get to know the current status of your new ministry before upsetting anyone's apple cart. Begin by only fixing what's clearly broken.

This will help you earn the trust of your team as you lay a foundation for bigger changes.

2. **Cast vision conversationally.** It's important that you lay a firm foundation of trust before instituting changes in ministry culture. It is wise to start by introducing language that helps bring clarity to the purpose of your ministry. For instance, if you see the main focus of your ministry as evangelistic, begin to regularly talk about reaching, teaching, and connecting with kids and families in your community. Emphasize the importance of teachers learning to share the gospel in a clear and simple way, and equip leaders with classroom resources to keep the gospel message at their fingertips. Be cautious to not merely place tasks on your teachers. You need to model your mission for them to see.

3. **Set vision intentionally.** When you are ready to draft your vision/official mission/purpose statement and set ministry goals, gather key members of your team together, and work through your vision with them. Since you have already been casting your vision conversationally, much of this discussion will center on clarifying the language that best describes your shared vision for the purpose of your ministry. Don't expect to get this done in a one-hour session. This process of crafting a mission statement will take time. It may merit a short retreat to get away from distractions and find focused and prayerful time to intentionally draft your statement.

4. **Share vision congregationally.** Once you have decided on a direction and have drafted mission, vision, and values statements, look for opportunities

to cast your vision for the entire church. Look for opportunities to communicate your mission through the church's various channels, like newsletters, blogs, Facebook pages, and from the pulpit. Sharing your mission with the whole of the congregation will help garner broader buy-in and may help in recruiting new helpers with whom your vision resonates.

5. **Display your vision environmentally.** Once your statement has been unveiled, post your *why* statement in places where it can be elevated and celebrated. Paint it on the walls of your children's wing, plaster it on posters, print it on T-shirts for your team to wear, and display on your newsletters, website, and social media outlets. Use your *why* as branding for your ministry.

6. **Live your vision consistently.** Of course, the most important aspect of having strong mission, vision, and values statements for your ministry is living it out. The best way to display your written purpose statements is to make decisions and function in accordance with the statements you have written. When you display your mission with your actions, it will become more than a statement of your values—it will become part of your church's culture.

What about Leading Change?

by Chuck Peters

Leading a ministry team through change is one of the most challenging things a leader must do. Change, especially when initiated by someone else, is hard for people. It threatens the status quo, activates a stress response, and causes people to react in fear. This is often the case because past change has not gone well. What people fear the most is uncertainty. When faced with the choice of a poor situation that is known and understood or an unknown situation that may be better, most people are content to stick with the known—albeit worse—situation. Put simply, people don't know what they like—they like what they know. Change-oriented leaders, especially new leaders who are change-minded, represent a major threat to people who are comfortable with the status quo.

Creating change in your ministry is like taking people on a journey. You need to tell them where you want to go, convince them that the destination is worth the trip, and invite them to join you on the journey. As you set out on the change journey to improve a ministry, it is wise to do so with patience, tact, and sensitivity for those who are along for the ride. That's not to say that you can't ever make changes quickly, just that you would be wise to first weigh the balance of making speedy changes with the potential fallout that may result in a loss of relational capital. You may enter a new role with a surplus of support and a figurative blank check in regards to making changes to a certain degree, but you must determine what amount of latitude you have to institute changes without inviting unwanted backlash. In the long run, the most important currency you can have in leading change is trust; and trust cannot be credited to you, it must be earned.

So where do you begin, and how long might it take to create the lasting cultural change that you desire? Here are four steps to help guide you as you guide your ministry through change:

Step 1. Accentuate the Positive. The church needs to know the trip will be enjoyable.

In winning people over, it is important to lead with positivity. The leader who continually harps on the shortcomings of an operation or who repeatedly points out problems will have a hard time gaining support in leading change. It is important to honor the past and respect the present as you press toward the future. Leaders must engage both the hearts and minds of their constituents to gain trust and credibility. There's a difference between leading and pushing. The cowboy drives with a whip and a loud voice. The cattle run because he scares them. A shepherd walks in front of his flock and calls the sheep by name. They follow because they trust him. People want to be part of things that are enjoyable. Make sure you set a positive tone as you integrate into the culture of your church/ministry.

Step 2. Assess the Situation. They need to know that you care.

Before you make any changes at all, it is important for you to learn the people, systems, and key assumptions of how things operate by personal experience. It is wise to begin with a learning period of six to nine months. During this time your primary goal is not to make any major changes, but to integrate yourself into the current way of doing things. As you do, you can determine what you have to work with and form your own opinions in regard to how things are going. This is a time to take inventory. List the assets you have to work with—including facility spaces, teaching tools and resources, supplies, and team members—and rate their condition/effectiveness. Also identify anything you might consider a liability—including facility spaces, teaching tools and resources, supplies, and team members—as you seek to establish a more healthy and effective children's ministry. Begin with basics and essentials: Make sure everything functions; only fix what's broken. And ask lots of "why" questions as you evaluate what's being done. *Why do we have this space set up this way? Why do we meet at this time? Why does he or she teach that age children?* Seek to build strong relationships with key influencers and contributors and earn the trust of your team, the staff, and parents in the church as you slowly begin to cast a vision for larger changes. People do not care what you know until they know that you care.

Step 3. Determine a Destination. They need to know where you want to go.

A good leader identifies a credible destination and a viable way to get there. Before instituting change, it is essential that you first clarify the *why* of your ministry—for yourself and for your team. When you are able to put words to the clear mission, vision, values, and purpose of your ministry, and can create language that describes your goal (where you want to go), you can lead with confidence that your decisions align with your destination. Your *why* is so important because it serves as both a target and a filter in regard to decision-making. Determining a destination is akin to beginning with the end in mind. If you do not know where you are going, how will you know you are going the right direction? How will you know when you have arrived? Describe and document the characteristics of the ministry you would like to build, then map out a route to get there. By describing the destination and identifying landmarks to mark the way, you can track progress to see how far you have come and know how much farther there is to go. When you cast vision for a desirable destination, people will be excited to go with you, even if the road is occasionally bumpy.

Step 4. Act without Hesitation. They need to know that you are committed to the cause.

Once you know where you are going and have buy-in from your team, keep your eyes set on the goal and drive there with confidence. Be intentional to avoid sidetracks and detours. Every action you take should advance your progress toward your destination. This requires planning, preparation, and discipline. You cannot wing it. You need to be purposeful to count the cost and stay the course. Knowing where you are going allows you to be confident, decisive, and clear-headed as you make decisions. If someone brings you a new idea of something they think you should do, you can quickly assess the request to see if it lines up with your map to bring you closer to where you want to go, or takes you off course. Leading with such confidence helps you to remain action-oriented, avoid procrastination, and communicate quickly in response to any inquiry.

The ultimate goal of leading change is to create a ministry that is clear in mission and purpose, and driven by a common culture that permeates the church. Influencing culture takes longer than dictating change, but cultural changes last longer and hold stronger

CHAPTER 2

DO THE DETAILS MATTER?

MANAGING MINISTRY SPECIFICS

Introduction

The little things really do mean a lot.

There are lots of plates to spin in kids ministry. When I started as a children's minister, I was responsible for all children, birth through sixth grade. As most of you know, that's a lot. I was constantly being torn between the needs of preschoolers and their families, and the unique needs of preteens and their families (and everything in between). I quickly realized that organization was my best friend.

When I was organized and had taken the time to think through specific roles and details of my ministry, I was fine. But, as soon as I let my guard down and allowed business to get in the way of managing the specifics, I was in trouble. The little things really did mean a lot, and it was often the little things that upset ongoing ministry.

In this chapter we're hoping to help you focus on some of the details we've seen kids ministry leaders forget. We're focusing on roles and responsibilities that can really make or break you. You might be tempted to skip over these questions because of their "administrative" nature, but don't. Satan doesn't want you to give attention to anything of kingdom value, even the tiniest details. So, don't allow him a stronghold, even over the little details. God cares about the details.

What about Administration?

---

by Chuck Peters

You probably got into kids ministry because you have a passion for communicating the truth of God's Word to children. People who are drawn to careers in kids ministry are often gifted at leading classroom sessions that center around teaching, storytelling, creative facilitation of crafts and hands-on learning activities, and building relationships with children. Chances are, you feel a sense of calling to kids ministry because you have been bestowed with the gift of communication and connection with kids, and when you work within your giftedness you are energized.

When gifted teachers transition into full-time kids ministers, however, many discover that the job they believed would be exhilarating is instead exhausting. Most in this category do not know exactly why they feel unsatisfied, but I have a theory. I believe many kids ministers struggle with dissatisfaction because they spend only a small portion of their time interacting with children.

It is important to take an eyes-wide-open approach that allows you to see where your time goes. The best way to do this is to keep a daily log of your activities, noting how much time each task takes, and then assess what you find. Performing a time study will help you see what you are currently doing, and it will help you identify areas that are taking more time than they should, and others that need more of your attention. Begin by taking a few moments to evaluate your typical workweek, estimating from memory, using this list of task categories:

- Meetings
- Teaching Preparation
- Leadership Investment
- Activity Preparation

- Discipleship
- Training
- Events
- Planning
- Prayer
- Volunteer Enlistment

How many hours per week do you spend in each of these areas? Feel free to add to this list or remove categories as you like. You can do this on paper, but I recommend using a spreadsheet (like Google Sheets or Microsoft Excel) so you can generate a chart to visualize the results. After entering your hours, click and drag to select the fields and generate a pie chart based on the data you entered.

Most leaders find that they spend less than 10 percent of their time interacting directly with children, and 90 percent of their time doing other tasks that we might categorize as administrative in nature. If you're motivated by teaching kids and drained by administrative work, you will no doubt feel some amount of frustration in the role. Fortunately, I have a good word for these leaders!

Let's first acknowledge that both teaching and administration are essential for ministry. In 1 Corinthians 12, the apostle Paul includes administration as one of the spiritual gifts that God gives for the building up of the church. Administration is, therefore, something that we would do well to embrace, whether we have the gift or not.

Why? In short, administration is a ministry multiplier. Administration is defined as the management of an office, business, or organization. It implies giving leadership, oversight, and guidance to other people. In the context of ministry this includes things like creating strategy, casting mission and vision, stewarding resources, and controlling policies and procedures. Administrating your ministry implies taking ownership, initiative, and responsibility for everything that happens in your area, including teaching kids and leading your adult team members. It includes all the work that you do in the office between "Sundays." It's about planning and preparation and prayer. The reality is, the work you do *between* Sundays greatly impacts the work you do *on* Sundays.

So what can you do in light of this need for administrative acumen? Here are five tips to help you find more satisfaction as you administrate your ministry:

1. **Accept it.** The notion that there is more to children's ministry than teaching is, in fact, a fact. What happens in the classroom during service times is the tip of the iceberg. Few people are aware of how much work happens behind the scenes in the in-betweens. As a kids minister, you need to be aware that the biggest part of your job, and the most important aspects of running a successful, vibrant ministry, will happen between Sundays.

2. **Adjust your expectation.** The next step is to adjust your expectation in regard to what your job "should" be like. In a forty-plus-hour workweek, you will likely spend less than four hours interacting directly with kids. As ministries grow, many kids ministry professionals find that they spend less and less time interacting directly with kids; some do not teach at all. Instead of thinking of yourself as a teacher of kids, think of yourself as a teacher of teachers and a leader of leaders. This mentality allows you to view your role in the proper perspective—you are a multiplier. That's the job.

3. **Take control of your calendar.** You can alter the balance of where your time goes by taking greater control over your calendar. Instead of reacting to each need

that arises through the day, take a proactive posture on your workweek. Schedule your work for each day, block time on your calendar for each task you need to take on, and stick to your schedule. If a job takes more time than it was allocated, add more time somewhere else. By planning your work and working your plan, you will find that you can feel a greater sense of control over your time.

4. **Lean into administration.** There is much more to kids ministry than teaching. Administration is leadership. It involves vision casting, goal setting, strategic planning, coordination of communication, training of leaders, and management of resources. Success in these areas will greatly increase the effectiveness of what happens during your teaching times.

5. **Recruit for it.** If you discover that you truly struggle in areas of administration, don't lose heart. Ministry is not meant to be done alone—it takes a team. If administration is a weakness for you, look to recruit a partner in ministry that is strong where you are weak. Chances are, there are people in your church who do have the gift of administration. By finding and recruiting one or more of them, you can reap great reward in the administrative area.

By learning to love the administrative side of your job, you will find that you can grow the influence, effectiveness, and efficiency of your ministry exponentially. When you do have the opportunity to teach kids directly, focus your attention on that special time and enjoy it to the full.

What about My Role on Church Staff?

by Jeff Land

Understanding your role at the church where you serve will greatly impact your fulfillment and satisfaction with your ministry. Every church is different; therefore, every church will have different ideas about the responsibilities that are expected of the kids ministry leader. Your church has likely provided you with a job description, and it covers the major expectations that you are responsible for fulfilling. At the bottom of that job description, there is likely a line that says "and other duties as assigned."

Those other duties are really where confusion can start. It's important that you quickly determine what other duties were not outlined on the job description. Much confusion can happen when you don't realize that in addition to being the ministry leader, you are also the "chief childcare coordinator" or that you are also responsible for hiring (and firing) of the weekday education staff.

Below are some helpful items to remember as you consider your role on church staff:

- **To whom do you report?** Churches aren't bureaucracies, but with the number of bosses you might feel like you have, it certainly can feel like it. Generally, all staff members report to the Senior Pastor or Executive Pastor; however, you may have some other bosses in the line. It's common for kids ministers to be led by a minister in a lead educational role. You will often find that you will answer to a personnel committee or board of elders or deacons as well.

- **How do I support my pastor?** It's important that you are supportive of your pastor. The pastor is responsible for leading the body that you serve. Supporting your pastor doesn't mean you will always agree with him or even always get along with him. Being supportive means that you will make a guarded effort to always speak kindly of your pastor in public settings, support the ministry causes he views as important, and support the vision that he has for the church. If you are in a position where you find you cannot support your pastor, it might be time for you to consider moving on to a new ministry at a different church.

- **How do I interact with other staff members?** Every church staff is different. Some church staffs operate as a cohesive unit, and other church staffs operate in silos. First, determine what type of staff you are serving on. If your church's ministries are siloed, you should do your part to make sure that everyone is aware of what's going on in the kids ministry and ask for help when needed. Likewise, offer help when other ministries have special events. Hopefully, the staff at your church will operate with a unified vision. If this is the case, do your part to help support that vision with the programming and curriculum that you offer. You will likely find staff members you connect with better—and that's okay. But try to avoid being exclusive. It's best for the church when all staff members are working together.

- **What if I'm a lay staff leader?** Being a volunteer ministry director can be difficult. Navigating the boundaries of what you are expected to do and what you are willing to do can be a seemingly impossible task. Be sure to talk with the pastor and ask him to define your role with the paid church staff as well as the congregation. By him vesting authority in your leadership, you will find that people will be more apt to follow you. Try to limit the amount of responsibility you take on to what you can handle, outside your daily responsibilities to your own family and work, so you can avoid burning out.

Ministry relationships can be some of the most rewarding and long-lasting relationships you will ever build. Joining together with other people who share a common interest in carrying out a vision together builds camaraderie. Serving on church staff can also be a lonely place, so building trusting relationships with fellow staff members can help greatly.

> It's important that you are supportive of your pastor.

What about Safety and Security?

by Delanee Williams

Parents want to know their child is in a safe and secure environment at church. Before we can even teach boys and girls biblical truths, we must earn the trust of the parents. We must do everything possible to keep children safe, secure, and happy while at church. This is a most important, basic responsibility for kids ministry leaders. Parents need to have peace of mind, knowing the church has specific guidelines to protect their child at church. Use the guidelines listed below to help maintain a safe and secure environment. Refer to the next section in this chapter regarding policies for additional information.

Safety

Food Safety

- Allergies can be a matter of life and death for some children. Provide an information sheet for parents to complete, stating the child's allergy, describing the allergic reaction, and detailing the emergency action plan if the child has a reaction. Communicate the information to the child's teachers. Be mindful not to serve any food that could lead to a child having an allergic reaction.
- Whenever food is used in the classroom for a snack or learning activity, post an allergy alert sign outside the classroom door.
- Ensure foods used for snacks and learning activities aren't a choking hazard.

First Aid

- Have a stocked first-aid kit available for teachers' use. Remember to keep it out of reach of preschoolers and children.
- Keep an up-to-date list of adults trained in CPR and first aid/choking.

Environment

Building

- Establish a welcome desk manned with an adult while children are at church.

- Have one entry and exit into the preschool and/or children's area (not including the fire emergency exits) for safety.
- Keep hallways and stairwells clutter free and well lit. Make sure passageways aren't blocked.
- Easily identify classrooms.
- Doors to the classrooms should have small windows in or beside them so classes can be observed at all times.
- Provide adequate square footage:
  - ❖ 35 sq. ft. per preschooler (babies–kindergarten)
  - ❖ 25 sq. ft. per child (1st–6th grades)
- Have a phone near the classrooms. Post emergency numbers nearby.

Classroom

- Maintain adequate teacher-to-child ratios (with the minimum of two adults):
  - ❖ Babies: 1:2
  - ❖ One- and two-year-olds: 1:3
  - ❖ Three- and four-year-olds: 1:4
  - ❖ Kindergarten: 1:5
  - ❖ 1st–6th grades: 1:6
- In preschool classrooms, cover electrical plugs.
- Lock cabinets and drawers in younger preschool classes.
- Keep the waste container out of reach of younger preschoolers.
- Place cleaning supplies out of reach of preschoolers and children.
- Regularly check furnishings, toys, and equipment for unsafe parts or areas.

- Post emergency procedures in the same location in each classroom.
- Check windows and doors to make sure nothing can get around a child's neck or cause harm to a child.
- Make sure outside doors are secured.
- Ensure door and cabinet handles are secure.
- Cover sharp edges in younger preschool rooms.
- Return supplies to the supply area to maintain an uncluttered classroom.
- If using plants in the classroom, only use plants that do not pose a danger to children.

Furniture

- Use appropriate size furniture for the children in the classroom.
- Anchor or secure any furniture that could fall or injure a child.

Toys

- Select toys for the age and developmental needs of the children in the class.
- Clean and disinfect toys after each teaching session.
- Use toys that aren't a choking hazard and are free from small parts.

Security

Establish screening procedures for all adults who work with minors in the church. Consider the following:

- Determine how long the adult needs to be a member before being allowed to serve.

- Require each person to complete a formal application giving permission for a background check and providing references. Complete a local, state, and federal check. Follow up with references. Repeat the screening process for each teacher every two to three years.
- Conduct personal interviews.
- Provide training for all volunteers related to sexual abuse, safety, and explanation of all policies and procedures.
- Choose a method for identifying approved leaders in the preschool and children's areas such as nametags or shirts.
- Staff each class with two unrelated adults (eighteen years of age or older) at all times. If two adults serving are related, add a third unrelated adult to the class.
- Consider securing video monitoring in public places.
- Adopt and adhere to a security system for parents dropping off and picking up children, such as a matching sticker. Include a sign-in sheet to communicate the parents' location and an avenue to communicate with them.
- Keep an accurate count of the children in each classroom.
- Establish regular safety and security checks throughout the children's area.
- Check with your insurance company for additional information related to safety and security.

The Lord has blessed us with the opportunity to teach and minister to children and their families. Safety and security are integral to any kids ministry; therefore, we must do our best to keep the children and teachers in our ministry safe and secure.

What about Policies and Procedures?

by Delanee Williams

Creating written policies and procedures may not be the most exciting part of kids ministry, but it is essential. Written policies and procedures protect the children, parents, leaders, and the church. They ensure the church is prepared to minister to children and their families.

Jesus loved and cared for the children. He valued them. We, too, should value children and provide them with the best care possible. Parents deserve to know their children are in a safe environment with their needs and the opportunity to learn the Bible. Teachers deserve to know they are supported and have quality materials and resources as they teach. The church deserves the best opportunity to reach and minister to children and their families.

Follow the steps below when developing and writing policies and procedures.

- **Pray.** At the beginning and throughout the process, pray. Pray for the Lord's protection over the ministry and for wisdom.
- **Enlist a team.** Developing the policies and procedures your church needs is a large undertaking, and it will be beneficial to gather a team together to accomplish the task. Include church members who bring different perspectives to the group and are invested in the children's ministry. Each of these following individuals can bring valuable information to the process:
  - ❖ A couple of parents invested in your ministry
  - ❖ Children's ministry teacher
  - ❖ Preschool ministry teacher

- ❖ Healthcare professional or medical personnel
- ❖ Emergency responder such as a firefighter or police officer
- ❖ Children's minister or director

- **Research.** Visit with other kids ministers, churches, and school districts in your area. Learn from their experiences and what policies and procedures they have in place. Become familiar with the local and state laws that can affect your church's policies and procedures. Consult your church's insurance company. Given their expertise, they may have insight, resources, and even possible sample policies to help in this process. Keep in mind, your church's policies may be similar to other churches in your area, but not exactly the same—each church is unique, so you must be careful to do what works for your church.

- **Determine the policies and procedures your church needs.** Consider the needs of the children while they are at church and church events. Keep in mind some policies will be specific to preschoolers and children, while others may be general, covering all ages of children.

- Some examples may include:[3]
    - ❖ General Policies:
        - ▼ Age of children and how they are assigned to classrooms
        - ▼ Availability of facilities, including childcare policies
        - ▼ Hours for church programming
        - ▼ The church's philosophy on the importance of teaching children
        - ▼ Curriculum used for Bible teaching

- ❖ Security Policies:
    - ▼ Security procedures for dropping off and picking up children any time they are at church or a church event (and how it operates), including the education of parents and teachers
    - ▼ Emergency and evacuation procedures
    - ❖ Fire Evacuation
    - ▼ Lost Child
    - ▼ Shelter in place (weather related)
    - ▼ Intruder/active shooter
    - ▼ Determine how and when teachers and parents will be notified if an emergency plan is being activated.
- ❖ Parent Policies/Guidelines:
    - ▼ Suggestions of items to bring for babies and younger preschoolers and how they should be labeled
    - ▼ Information about toys that should be left at home
    - ▼ Completion of the sign-in sheet
    - ▼ Procedures for checking on their children during the session
- ❖ Teacher Policies/Guidelines:
    - ▼ The enlistment, screening, training, and supervision of teachers
    - ▼ Background checks on all volunteers or employed teachers who work with minors
    - ▼ Teacher-to-child ratios
    - ▼ A minimum of two unrelated adult (eighteen years or older) teachers with the children at all times.

- ▼ Six-month rule (teachers must have been members of the church at least six months before they can begin teaching)
- ▼ Consider additional policies and outlined expectations if your ministry meets in a shared space
- ❖ Health, Hygiene, and Infectious Disease Policies/Guidelines:
  - ▼ When and how to wash hands (teachers and children)
  - ▼ When and how to disinfect toys, teaching resources, furniture, and other objects
  - ▼ Diapering and toileting procedures
  - ▼ How to handle spills of bodily fluids (urine, nasal secretions, blood, etc.)
  - ▼ Wellness policy: list of common symptoms when a child will not be allowed to attend church activities and events
  - ▼ Procedures if a child becomes sick while at church
  - ▼ Informing a parent of a sick child
  - ▼ Responding to a medical emergency
  - ▼ Proper records of children's allergies and steps to take if a child has an allergic reaction
- ❖ Child Abuse Policies:
  - ▼ Setting up training for recognizing child abuse
  - ▼ Developing procedures for reporting child abuse and responding after child abuse has been reported

- ▼ Informing parents, volunteers, and staff of the legal procedures and requirements regarding child abuse cases
- ❖ Playground Policies/Guidelines:
  - ▼ Equipment inspections, maintenance, and safety protocols
  - ▼ Supervision of children
- Consider including the items below with the written policies and procedures:
  - ❖ A greeting from the pastor, children's minister, and/or children's ministry team
  - ❖ The purpose for the policies
  - ❖ The church's and children's ministry mission statements
  - ❖ Contact information of church if parents or teachers have questions

Make a first draft of your policies and review it. Work toward being concise, but thorough. The policies need to be clear, but remember, if they are too long, parents and teachers may not read them. Brief paragraphs and bullet points of information are helpful. Your team may decide to have a shorter version for parents with the information that specifically pertains to them.

Have your church lawyer or legal counsel, insurance company, and healthcare professional look over the policies and procedures to make suggestions. More than likely, you'll want to make additions and changes to the document after hearing their suggestions.

- **Seek buy-in and gather feedback.** Share copies of the draft with a select group of teachers, parents, and church staff. Communicate that this is a draft and seek their input. By getting their feedback, they are more likely to follow and support the policies and procedures.

- **Finalize the document and make it official.** Revise the draft to make the necessary changes and follow your church's process for making the policies and procedures official.
- **Communicate.** Once the plans are written, educate parents, teachers, and other church members. Decide how the information will be shared and communicated to the church. Recognize some policies may need to be highlighted or revised from time to time in the future as situations arise in your church or in society. Determine how new parents and teachers will receive a copy and learn of the church's policies and procedures.
- **Train leaders.** Remember to include training for teachers regarding the policies and procedures. After an initial training, regularly remind teachers of the procedures. Plan ongoing trainings throughout the year and highlight a specific policy or procedure during each training. Consider keeping a written copy in each classroom for teachers' quick reference.

Review the policies and procedures periodically. Ensure information is up-to-date and add any additional information if needed. Make sure to communicate with teachers and parents if any changes have been made.

CHAPTER 3

WHAT TOOLS DO I NEED?

SHARPENING YOUR MINISTRY BASICS

Introduction

It was late spring in Nashville, and the hydrangeas were in full bloom. A certain kids ministry leader was envious, jealous, and yes, borderline coveting his neighbor's displays of God's handiwork. So I—I mean *he*—took off to the local nursery to purchase not one, but two fully bloomed, three-gallon potted hydrangeas. When returning home to plant the incredible specimens, it was quickly discovered that said kids ministry leader didn't own a shovel—a very important tool if you plan to plant anything in Tennessee dirt.

There are certain tools we all need to have available to us in kids ministry. Tools that we need to keep in our toolbox and use when needed. Too many kids ministry leaders think they have to create everything themselves and "dig holes" with no shovel when there are really good shovels readily available.

This chapter is dedicated to sharing several tools that you can use in your ministry—tried-and-true programing and resources that can make a huge difference as you implement your ministry to boys and girls and their families. At LifeWay Kids we are committed to serving the church in her mission of making disciples. We are committed to trustworthy content, rooted in Scripture. We hope you'll take a look at our "tools," but more so, we want to encourage you to look at all resources with a careful eye. Look beyond the cover to see what's really inside.

This garden story ends with a best friend loaning an over-anxious kids minister his very nice shovel. We'll see if the plants return next season.

What about Physical Environment?

by Bill Emeott

Does the size of our classrooms really matter? Do the lighting, room temperature, and cleanliness affect what happens in the room? YES!

Let's start here: not everyone has a state-of-the-art, brand new, cool, and exciting space. In fact, many of us are in buildings that were designed and built fifty years ago. Don't be frustrated. Be thankful for what you have and make the most of every inch.

Perhaps you've been given the task of designing or remodeling new space for your ministry. What a blessing! Creating and maintaining a positive physical environment is essential to effective learning—give the impression that what happens in that space is important. It's not only important to you and the kids and families you serve, but attention to the physical environment says that kids ministry is important to the kingdom.

Consider these tips for creating a good physical learning environment in your kids ministry:

First Impressions

It's been said before and it's worth hearing again: "You only get one chance to make a first impression." When visitors enter your church and your kids ministry space, what do they see? How do they feel? What impression does your physical space give?

We often become immune to our own environment. We don't see (or smell) our own mess. A good way to begin evaluating

> "You only get one chance to make a first impression."

your space is to ask a friend (perhaps someone who doesn't attend your church) to give you an honest—painfully honest, if necessary— impression of your space. Give full permission for honesty, then listen and take notes. Hear her observations. After she's shared, ask, "Based on what you've seen and observed, what importance and value do you believe this church puts on kids ministry?"

That's a great place to start.

Colors Matter

Choosing the right color (or colors) for your space affects the environment. Too dark can make your space seem small, and too bright can over stimulate and create a feeling of anxiety. Primary colors tend to lose their appeal after a short period of time. Choose soft, gender-neutral colors in infant rooms, and slowly add deeper tones in older kids' spaces. Jewel-tone accent walls and splashes of color will create a modern, exciting feel.

Space Recommendations

When considering room and furniture recommendations, there are some standards to strive toward. Remember your reality, but knowing the standard can help you make informed decisions.

Location

Avoid a layout that requires people to walk through to get to another part of the building. If possible, there should be one way in and one way out to provide a secure environment. Consider placing preschool space as close to where parents meet as possible.

Recommended Square Footage:

- 35 sq. ft. per person in a preschool classroom (maximum attendance of twelve)
- 25 sq. ft. per person in a younger elementary classroom (maximum attendance of sixteen)
- 20 sq. ft. per person in an older elementary classroom (maximum attendance of twenty-four)

Doors

Classroom doors should have a small glass view panel to allow monitoring of classroom activities. Such doors help to assure the safety and security of those inside.

Flooring

Use flooring that can be cleaned thoroughly. Carpets with thick pads can be a problem because they hold moisture, bacteria, and odors. Vinyl tile is a good basic flooring that is easily maintained. Adding removable rugs that can be cleaned or replaced in younger preschool rooms is recommended.

Chairs and Tables

- Ones/Twos = seat is 10 inches from the floor
- Threes–Kindergarten = seat is 12 inches from the floor
- Younger Kids = seat is 12–15 inches from the floor
- Older Kids = seat is 15–17 inches from the floor
- Tables should be 10 inches above the chair seat.

Whiteboards and Bulletin Boards

Whiteboards can be a great addition to kids space if there is a use for them. If you don't really need it and don't plan to use it, don't mount it! However, both whiteboards and bulletin boards should be mounted where the center of the board is at the child's eye level.

Consider the kids who will use that room—who are expected to see what's on those boards—and mount accordingly.

Temperature and Lighting

Rooms should be neither too hot nor too cold. An appropriate temperature for learning is 70–75 degrees Fahrenheit. Use an appropriate level of lighting, as kids function best in brightly lit rooms. Natural lighting has an impact on learning, so introduce natural light with ample windows whenever possible.

Use of Technology

Equipping kids ministry space with new technology is only valuable if the investment will be used. Consider curriculum options and recommendations. Consider teacher preference and understanding. Remember that just because you *can* doesn't mean you *should*. Never allow new technology to replace relationships. Never encourage new technology at the risk of good teaching. Use technology to enhance the learning experience and good teaching.

> Never allow new technology to replace relationships.

Permanently mounted screens and accessories are always preferred over those that might fall and potentially injure kids. Again, consider the location and height based on use and kids' eye levels. Avoid mounting anything that can become a hazard.

What about All the Stuff?

In most teaching environments, less is more. Don't be confused: clutter does not equal good teaching. While there can be a lot of "stuff," it doesn't all have to be out at the same time. Closed cabinets and shelving can store unneeded resources and help create an inviting, clean environment.

Baby and toddler rooms should be furnished sparingly. Leave plenty of room for movement. Rockers, beds, changing tables, and a soft, carpeted area to crawl and toddle are important. Most toys should be cleanly stored and brought out as needed. Too many toys at one time can create a mess and leave babies and toddlers overwhelmed. Two or three at a time will work just fine.

- Preschool classrooms require more resources. Create learning spots/areas where different class activities can take place. Use tablecloths on the floor, masking tape, or furnishings to designate different areas.

- Elementary space can be limited to appropriately heightened chairs, tables, and open bookshelves, leaving open space for active games and activities. Closed cabinetry is desired for supplies that are unique to a classroom but not intended to be accessible to kids each week.

- Resource rooms or closets provide storage for consumable resources that everyone needs (construction paper, glue, markers, crayons, etc.) and space to store needed-but-seldom-used resources (themed puzzles, preschool toys that are available to bring into a room upon occasion, etc.).

Is it clean? Is it bright and inviting? Has attention been given to safety and security? Or does it smell? Is it cluttered with unneeded furniture and outdated teaching supplies and resources? If you answered yes to either of the last two questions, it's probably time to purge, clean, and use these suggestions to give your space a makeover.

What about Programming and Events?

by Jeff Land

Everyone loves a good party, right? Well, maybe not everyone. Planning events in children's ministry can be a fun but daunting task. Ministry leaders can sometimes be placed in different categories based on their approach to ministry. Each leadership style has different strengths they bring to the event-planning table.

- **Cruise Director:** The *cruise director* children's minister is full of ideas for events. She's constantly got the next event in motion. Sometimes she even double-books events. Her events are often poorly planned and can sometimes be chaotic.

- **Drill Sergeant:** The *drill sergeant* children's minister likes organization. He will often have every detail of the event planned out. This leader will know exactly what time each part of the event will begin and will have every permission slip signed and in alphabetical order. Generally, the only thing missing from his events is . . . FUN! They are so structured that kids often get overlooked in the details.

- **Teacher:** The *teacher* children's minister loves to plan events as long as they have some educational point. The events will be well executed and generally involve a themed snack, craft to reinforce the point, and a game if the kids are good. The teacher is an excellent planner, but will often overlook good opportunities for events because he can't see the educational value.

- **Coach:** The *coach* children's minister will do anything for some good friendly competition. All of her events will feature games, and kids will be placed on teams. Competitive kids thrive at these events because they speak directly to their personalities. Kids who are not as competitive will often be seen in little huddles around the outside of game areas.

- **Factory Worker:** The *factory worker* children's minister has every event down to a science. He has done the same events every year for the length of his ministry. Over the years, with very few tweaks, the minister pulls off each event like clockwork using the same decorations, same menus, and even the same volunteers. The younger kids might look forward to the events as rites-of-passage, but older kids become tired of the same old thing.

Reading through the above list, you might have found yourself identifying with one or more of the different types of ministry leaders. It's okay—there's not a "right" one. There are, however, some important takeaways in each of the styles. Here are some *dos* and *don'ts* that might help you as you plan your event calendar:

- Cruise Director: *Do* keep things interesting. Be on the lookout for new trends and current recreational events that kids enjoy being a part of. *Don't* halfway plan more events than are necessary, or more events than you can pull off with excellence.
- Drill Sergeant: *Do* pay attention to details. If this isn't your gift, recruit someone to be on your team who can make sure that every detail has been attended to. *Don't* forget the fun! Remember: it's okay for kids to laugh and play.
- Teacher: *Do* plan some events each year with a specific focus. Help kids understand the point of why you are

doing the event. *Don't* think that a child has to take a trinket home from every event to prove to her mom that she "really did" something.

- Coach: *Do* plan fun games and activities. Kids love to play games. *Don't* put too much focus on winning. Be careful to not make any child feel left out.

- Factory Worker: *Do* repeat events that are successful. Determining events that minister to the kids in your church and community and repeating them annually is a great thing. *Don't* always do it the same way. It's okay to shake things up a little bit. Change up the decor, change up the theme, or change up the leadership. Just keep repeating to yourself . . . "Change is okay."

What about VBS?

by Melita Thomas

Vacation Bible School, or VBS, is synonymous with summer in many church settings. Why? Well, it could have something to do with the fact that it's been around in one form or another since 1898. In a setting such as kids ministry, which is often marked by trendy, short-lived fads, the question you're likely asking is: *Is a century-old strategy still an effective one? Is VBS relevant to today's kids?* You bet it is!

One of the best signs of VBS's health and stability is its longevity. Rather than being a sign of its irrelevance, VBS's longevity proves it is a dependable ongoing ministry. Very few things in kids ministry have that kind of staying power. It's a trusted resource and a successful strategy. In fact, VBS is used by more than twenty-five thousand churches each year to reach over 2.5 million people. Last year, more than seventy thousand salvation decisions were reported as a direct result of VBS. Talk about impact![4]

In one evangelical denomination, VBS consistently accounts for roughly 25 percent of all baptisms.[5] Think about that for just a second. One-quarter of all people reached by any of these churches are reached through VBS. That's a staggering statistic! If VBS were to suddenly disappear from these churches, what evangelistic strategy would take its place? VBS isn't just about fun and games (and crafts . . . and snacks). Its primary purpose is leading people to experience the life-transforming power of the gospel. That's a critically important function of the church. When viewed through the lens of the gospel, VBS takes on a renewed purpose.

> VBS's primary purpose is leading people to experience the life-transforming power of the gospel.

VBS is unique in that every aspect is intentionally designed to provide opportunities for age-appropriate evangelism. Every activity, every rotation, every song is specially crafted to fit the point of the day, making it possible for every person the child encounters throughout their VBS day to "live out" the gospel in front of them. That makes every job important. Snack ladies are no longer "just snack ladies." Recreation leaders are not just responsible for wearing kids out so that they can sit still and listen longer during Bible study. Each point of engagement becomes an opportunity to talk to a child about what the Bible teaches and about what the Holy Spirit might be saying to him or her.

Think of VBS as a "summer intensive." Parents might enroll their serious student or athlete in a summer intensive program that provides their kids an opportunity to immerse themselves in thorough training. This usually includes several hours of instruction and practice sessions every day over the course of several weeks. VBS is a similar experience in a child's spiritual development. Current research suggests that a child who is actively involved in church may actually only attend church one to two times a month, which translates into a couple of hours each month. A traditional VBS involves three hours a day for five days in a row. This is equivalent of seven months of "church" for today's typical church-going child! The opportunities for evangelism, discipleship, and relationship-building that can take place in one week of VBS might take half a year for a Sunday school teacher.

And when VBS is done right, the relationships don't end once VBS is over. VBS is the perfect opportunity to connect with children and families who might not otherwise attend church. It's fun and nonthreatening as a first exposure, and it gives kids an opportunity to develop a sense of ownership (my room, my teacher, my friends) that makes return visits easier. Hosting a VBS celebration or family night at the end of VBS allows parents within the church to reach out and make connections with parents outside the church. Again, intentionality is key.

> VBS is the perfect opportunity to connect with children and families who might not otherwise attend church.

Another strength of VBS is its flexibility and versatility. VBS is a completely customizable event. It can take place on-campus or off. It can be held in a backyard down the street, or on a mission trip around the globe. It can be closely or broadly graded. You can call it VBS, Adventure Week, Fun Zone, or whatever name you like best. Replace the rotations and use it as a sports camp or music and arts camp with a Bible study component. The sky's the limit! VBS is an opportunity to ignite the imagination of your church, involve volunteers and older students in the church's youth group in short-term commitments (positive experiences in VBS often lead to a desire to become more involved in kids ministry), and connect with the kids in your church and community.

Why should VBS be part of your summer strategy? It's flexible. It's dependable. It's fun. But most important, it has the opportunity to impact lives for eternity as kids, teens, and adults come to know the saving power of Jesus Christ. That alone makes VBS worth it!

What about Camp?

by Jeremy Echols

Camp Is a Mountaintop

We've all heard stories about that "one moment" at camp when there was a revival, an overflow of emotion, a special time of calling, a relationship was mended, and the Lord's presence was felt. It was the mountaintop, and those moments are powerful. Sometimes they can be anticipated, but many times they are spontaneous, unique, and powerful. Too many times, the experience ends when the group returns from camp.

Camp Can Be a Spiritual Market

The wise kids ministry leader will seek to take kids from having just a mountain-top experience to helping them recognize and commemorate a mile marker of spiritual growth so it is not just a one-time event. We see the importance in Scripture of spiritual milestones. When the Israelites crossed the Jordan River, God commanded them to set up twelve marker stones as a sign of His greatness and faithfulness. Joshua 4:21–24 says:

> "In the future, when your children ask their fathers,
> 'What is the meaning of these stones?' you should

tell your children, 'Israel crossed the Jordan on dry ground.' For the LORD your God dried up the water of the Jordan before you until you had crossed over, just as the LORD your God did to the Red Sea, which he dried up before us until we had crossed over. This is so that all the peoples of the earth may know that the LORD's hand is mighty, and so that you may always fear the LORD your God."

Wouldn't we all love to see kids form into fully devoted followers of Christ in just a week's time and a short van ride away? But we realize that in five days, no camp or curriculum can spiritually form kids. The role of camp is to cast vision for Christlike living, complement your ongoing kids ministry, and dive as deep as possible with a spiritual concept. A week of camp is valuable, but let's not ask it to be more than it can be.

Camp is not all that kids need, but milestones are important, and camp provides the perfect setting for kids to *get away, see for themselves,* and *learn the truth* about the greatness and faithfulness of the Lord.

Kids Get Away to Camp

- Retreat: Whether you plan your own camp or attend a camp like CentriKid that is designed to handle the programming for you, it is important to get away. Get kids out of their normal day-to-day routines. It can be healthy to change it up. The nature of a camp retreat is refreshing, and often when kids are away, they tend to hear the message or hear from God in a new way.
- Remove Distractions: Camp is a great time to connect relationally with kids in your ministry because camp is distraction-free. There are no cell phones, no

video games, no homework assignments, no sports team practices. With these distractions removed, you can build relationship and influence that lasts long into the year. At CentriKid, we encourage staff and church leaders to use meals, hang-out times, walks across campus, and late-night chats as opportunities to spend quality time and build real relationships.

- Go All-In: You can do things at camp that you just can't do at home or at church. Don't pass up the unique opportunities like shaving cream and water balloon wars. The recreational opportunities and friendships that can form through alliances in silly games can sometimes be a long-lasting takeaway that nobody suspected. God can use these childhood memories from camp to remind kids of spiritual truths later on when they need it most.

Kids See for Themselves at Camp

As a kids ministry leader, help kids make some of their best memories in the context of having fun with friends and talking about the things of God. Talk to campers about their Bible study sessions and what they learned and felt during worship. You can support their spiritual growth by helping campers recall the lessons from camp when they need them during school or at home.

Because the environment of camp is a safe place to try something new, many campers will attempt and fail, attempt and fail, and ultimately succeed at new things. This could be a physical activity they are learning at track time or spiritual milestones or questions a child is wrestling with. Campers are exploring on their own in an environment that is physically safe, emotionally safe, and spiritually safe. Every summer at CentriKid, I hear from church leaders about kids who opened up because they knew they could trust the staff and church leaders at camp.

Kids Learn Truth at Camp

All of the relationship-building, removal of distractions, and stretching beyond comfort zones is done for a reason: the time at camp allows kids to learn spiritual truths from the camp leaders, adults who are with them, and from their friends. Don't forget that they are learning and forming associations with spiritual truths even when they aren't in a "teaching time." Campers learn by the things we say, the attitudes we display, and the way we model our own spiritual lives in front of them.

As a leader, you have an opportunity to be part of the experience, but it takes effort and planning. After it's over, you also need to follow-up with kids from your group to help them continue to grow once they return home.

Camp is a gift that you can enjoy all year, because the spiritual impact and relationships last longer than just the week you are away. In fact, the week of camp is only the beginning for a kids ministry leader who is intentional about seeing kids grow in their walk with Christ.

What about Budgeting?

by Chuck Peters

No one likes budgets. We don't like them in our personal lives, and we don't enjoy having them imposed upon our ministries.

I believe this is because most people tend to think of budgets like speed limits—restrictions that prohibit us from driving as fast as we'd like to drive, or, in this case, from spending as much as we'd like to spend. However, a slight change of perspective can alter everything in regard to your relationship with your budget, both at church and at home.

The challenge is to think of your budget not as a limitation, but as an allocation. Thinking of your budget as an allowance feels more like a freedom than confinement, and can help you view the resources you have with fresh eyes. In reality, we have no choice but to work from a budget, so here are a few tips for operating from your budget effectively:

1. Know what you have. It is imperative that you know how much money is in your budget at the start of your fiscal year, and that you know when the fiscal year resets. There is typically a "budgeting season" that takes place before the start of the next fiscal year. This will be your time to make a case if you feel that you need to add money to your budget. If you intend to do this, however, make sure you can present a good case as to why additional funds may be needed and what result they may generate. Making requests for increased budgets may be as simple as drafting an e-mail, or may require making a formal presentation to a board.

2. Prioritize allocations. It is wise to start your year by allocating or earmarking funds that are needed for known recurring projects or resources. Your quarterly curriculum is likely a large portion of your budget, and is very likely a predictable cost allocation that you can set aside right out of the gate. Likewise, large annual events like VBS can be anticipated from the start, and it is wise for you to set aside funds in reserve for that purpose. Create a list of all of your known recurring expenses and divide out your money for these uses. You may need to allow for midweek Bible study resources, advancement gifts, craft and art supplies, and training for yourself and your leaders. Once you have outlined some categories and allocated dollars to each area, you can get a sense of how much you have left for discretionary spending through the year. You may do well to keep this list in a spreadsheet so you can list your quarterly and annual actuals next to your budgeted allocations to track variances and see which areas come in better or worse than your plan.

3. Know what you have spent. With a plan in place, you must next keep your eye on your remaining balance(s) throughout the year so that you always know how much you have to work with at any given time. It can be easy for spending to get out of control if you take your eye off your balance. It is smart to review your budget versus actual spending quarterly so that you can make adjustments depending on whether you are ahead of or behind your planned spending. If you are uber diligent, you may opt to update your budget/actual spreadsheet weekly so that you have a real-time view of each area.

4. Keep good records. In addition to a spreadsheet of dollars budgeted and actual dollars spent, keep a journal where you note spending decisions and strategies so that you can remember why you allocated or spent as you did when the next budgeting season rolls around. Too often we trust our fleeting memories, but they may fail us in regard to the kinds of details needed to set our budgets. A journal entry is a great way to log the thinking behind your spending. Likewise, keep your receipts organized and accessible so that you can review them yourself, or produce them for others if asked. Consider writing brief notes on each receipt to explain the purpose of the transaction. Some leaders make a practice of snapping a photo of each receipt with their phones and creating digital file folders where they can store virtual versions of their receipts.

5. Determine trends. You should find that you get better and better at predictive allocation of your budget with each new budget year. For example, watching attendance trends in your kids area has a direct influence on how you budget. You may have a very large group of kindergarteners one year that require more advancement gifts than in other years. Growth in attendance will have a direct and predictable impact on your annual VBS and quarterly curriculum resource needs.

More kids require additional resources, and that necessitates additional investment.

Managing your budget is an important part of your role as a leader. Stewarding your resources well, allocating funds accurately, and tracking spending trends will help you manage your budget efficiently and faithfully.

What about Grouping Kids?

by Tim Pollard

One of the more valuable tools you have when leading kids is wrapped around ideas you use to group the kids. This strategy honestly might vary depending on the type of environment you are using and the ages of kids involved. We'll take a look at a few strategies and think about times when those groupings might differ.

Several strategies exist for grouping kids in Bible study, and much of your decision may depend on the number of kids you have in your ministry. Here are the top two terms you might hear when you discuss grouping kids:

- **Closely Graded.** Closely graded simply means that kids are grouped in narrow-aged groupings instead of broad-aged groups, as we'll discuss next. For preschool classrooms, you'll want to check your local school district and start grouping kids around age 3 or 4 with kids who will be typically attending school at the same time. Some parents may choose to start their kindergarteners a year later depending on their age, and you can adjust those groupings as the needs arise.

- **Broadly Graded.** Broadly graded groupings are not as rigid as closely graded ones, since they aren't necessarily based on grade in school—but surely can be. Broadly graded groups may choose to group more on a child's understanding and ability than a specific grade range.

Here are a few times you might need to group kids and some considerations for choosing a grouping that best fits your kids and ministry:

Sunday Morning

- If you have enough volunteers and enough kids, you may want to group kids by school grade in a more closely graded format. Kids of the same age and school grade will be on a level playing field and may be able to learn better as they interact with their age-group peers.

- If you have smaller numbers of volunteers and kids, you may decide to group them into larger, broadly graded groups. You can refer to these groups by whatever naming convention you decide, but many choose general terms, such as "younger kids" and "older kids." As mentioned earlier, since these groupings are a bit more general, you can decide which kids belong in which group and may choose to group them based on abilities (walkers vs. non-walkers; readers vs. pre-readers, perhaps) instead of grade in school. School grade is still a good way to group, but consider grouping kids who are more alike in age and level of education, like first–third and fourth–sixth, if this is the strategy you choose. Your church may choose to group kindergarteners with either preschoolers or other elementary-age kids.

- Some churches with multiple services will choose both options, having closely graded options during the time frame with the most kids and broadly graded options during the other time frame with smaller groups of kids.

Midweek

If you have an evening program or a midweek program, you probably need to decide which type of grouping will work best for your intent for the program. Understand that the grouping could change from year to year depending on the breakdown of the ages of kids in the program, even if the intent of your program doesn't change.

VBS

Typically Vacation Bible School, or whatever you call your summer experience, will be more closely graded in nature because there will be larger numbers of kids and volunteers. In smaller churches, that won't always be the case, so there may be a need to have a more broadly graded approach.

Events

It is most likely that all of your events will be broadly graded. It really depends on the nature and purpose of your event as to how you might need to group your kids. Here are a few examples: Family events would likely not need to be grouped to begin with since parents and kids would be participating together. A tea party for girls would likely need to be graded by broadly aged groups. An amusement park event would be closely graded with multiple responsible adults taking a small group of same-age kids. Evaluate each event and decide for your group which strategy is best.

As you can see, there are two main strategies to consider when grouping kids. The real driving point for making that decision lies in the number of kids and the number of adult volunteers you have to accommodate the group. Don't be shy experimenting between the different strategies, and always be sure to evaluate your strategy each year in the event that it should be changed.

What about Curriculum?

by Landry Holmes

One of the most important decisions you make as a kids ministry leader is what curriculum materials to use. In theory, curriculum is more than pixels on a screen or words and pictures on a page. Curriculum includes the physical and emotional teaching-learning environments, equipment, consumable resources, teaching procedures, activity pages, posters, computers, tablets, television screens, etc. However, let's limit our conversation to digital or print teacher guides, learner guides, and related materials.

The first question to ask is, "What do I expect from my curriculum materials?" Curriculum is a tool and only a tool. The fanciest, coolest, prettiest curriculum will not teach kids the gospel, apart from the work of the Holy Spirit. The Spirit, through the message of Christ, gives kids new hearts. Curriculum can be a part of that process but on its own, can't do anything.

The second question is, "Does the curriculum content present the truth and nothing but the truth?" Jesus says in Matthew 28:19–20,

"Go, therefore, and make disciples of all nations, baptizing them in the name of the Father and of the Son and of the Holy Spirit, teaching them to observe everything I have commanded you. And remember, I am with you always, to the end of the age." Our ultimate goal is to make disciples of kids. The Bible is clear that making disciples includes teaching them the Bible.

Paul reminds his young protégé in 2 Timothy 2:15 to, "Be diligent to present yourself to God as one approved, a worker who doesn't need to be ashamed, correctly teaching the word of truth." This means that we present Bible content to kids without embellishment, always.

> Our ultimate goal is to make disciples of kids.

The kids alive during Bible times either experienced violence and hardship, or they heard stories about battles and God's provision. Some of them heard about the Messiah. Others sat in the Messiah's lap. They also memorized long passages of Scripture that didn't have any action in them. Do you think their parents and teachers embellished the stories of old to keep kids from being bored? Of course they didn't, and neither should we. If we think we have to add to the Bible content just to make it interesting to kids, what are we saying about our belief in God's inerrant Word?

A third question to ask is, "Does the curriculum content point kids to Jesus?" This may come as a surprise to many of us, but kids were around during Bible times! How do you think they learned about God's plan of redemption? They studied and were taught the Scriptures. Again, Paul reminds Timothy, "And you know that from infancy you have known the sacred Scriptures, which are able to give you wisdom for salvation through faith in Christ Jesus" (2 Tim. 3:15).

So, how do we determine if any given set of curriculum materials teaches God's truth unaltered and points kids to Jesus? To start with, you may want to enlist a team to help you evaluate current curriculum materials and choose curriculum for the future. Evaluation steps may include the following:

- Identify what program areas require curriculum materials:
  - ❖ Ongoing Bible Study?
  - ❖ Short-term Discipleship?
  - ❖ Vacation Bible School?
  - ❖ Missions Education?
  - ❖ Worship Hour?
- For each program area, determine the desired outcomes for your church's context.
- Evaluate your current curriculum materials to see if they equip teachers to meet those outcomes.
- If your current curriculum falls short, examine other curriculum options.

A lot of curriculum options are available today—some are free, some are expensive, and some are in between—so how do you discern what's best for your church? Evaluate each curriculum using objective criteria, such as the following:

- What is the foundation on which the curriculum is built?
  - ❖ Does the doctrinal stance of the curriculum provider align with and support your church's beliefs and mission?
  - ❖ Does the scope and sequence (or study plan) meet the desired outcomes referenced above?
  - ❖ Does the scope and sequence follow a wise discipleship plan?
- Is the content—including skits, video, music, and art—biblically accurate and appealing to kids?

- Does each teaching session point kids to Jesus?
- Is the teaching material age-appropriate? Does it help today's kids apply Bible truth?
- Does the curriculum provide resources for connecting church and home?
- Does the publisher provide the best value—not necessarily the lowest price?

Of course, you and your team may want to ask additional questions. Using a tool will help you evaluate all the curriculum choices consistently.[6]

Whatever route you take regarding the choice of curriculum materials, remember that kids deserve the best you can give them. While God can use any curriculum that contains Bible truth to teach kids the Bible, God expects us as leaders to choose materials that ultimately glorify Him.

> Kids deserve the best you can give them.

What about Technology?

by Melita Thomas

Modern technology has revolutionized the way we ingest and digest information. What once required voracious research is now instantly available with a few quick keystrokes or taps of the thumb. Seemingly limitless information is available to us. Technology even impacts the way we communicate with one another.

Regardless of your personal feelings about the benefits or drawbacks of modern technology in the classroom, today's kids are "digital natives" and fully immersed in it. They're not just comfortable with it—they have never known life without it. Because of this, kids ministry leaders may be tempted to think that they must weave multiple forms of technology into every experience in order to relate to or communicate effectively with kids.

But here's the reality. Technology is simply a tool—nothing more, nothing less. Even the sleekest, most cutting-edge bells and whistles cannot make up for a lack of preparation or passion on the part of the leader. And it is a poor substitute for personal relationships, so it should never eliminate the need for a "real, live teacher." However, as with most tools, when used effectively, it can be extremely useful in teaching God's Word to children.

Here are some key ways to harness the power of technology in kids ministry:

1. Use technology to build relationships with families. Texting, e-mail, and social media allow for "face time" with families outside of church. Social media helps you stay connected and know what is happening in the lives of families. E-mail is a great way to communicate with families and an easy way to remain accessible to them.

Some quick and easy ideas include:

- Sending quick notes of encouragement to parents
- Sending weekly (BRIEF!) parent updates with a summary of what was covered in Sunday school and some talking points to help parents continue a spiritual conversation at home
- E-newsletters, invitations, e-cards
- Sharing pictures from church activities with parents

Some cautions:

- Long e-mails are less likely to be read. Keep the content short and relevant.

- Tone of voice and intent can be difficult to interpret via electronic communication. Conduct sensitive or difficult conversations in person.

- Remember that e-mails, texts, and direct messages can be easily forwarded to people other than only the intended recipient(s).

- Follow your church's guidelines for communication with minors. Keep in mind that the "virtual world" has "real world" parallels. A good rule of thumb is to enforce your church's "real world" guidelines or policies in the virtual world as well. For example: Follow the two-person rule and always have more than one adult included in all electronic communication with a child. This keeps the conversation above board and protects volunteers from any false allegations. Above all, never communicate electronically with a child unless you have express permission from his or her parents.

2. Incorporate technology strategically in the classroom. Don't worry about staying on the cutting edge. Technology changes so rapidly it is almost impossible to keep up, and it can get expensive to continually update! Instead, look at each session for ways that make sense to use technology. Here are a few favorites:

- **Digital pictures**—Document and share activities and projects with kids and their families. This is especially great for things like blocks where the activity does not yield a product that can be taken home at the end of the session.

- **Presentations**—Lead kids to work together as a group to create and present information.

- **Music videos**—Incorporate existing videos in worship or encourage kids to make their own to express praise and worship.
- **DVD and downloaded video**—Whether available online or as part of your curriculum, videos can help kids visually experience the content being taught.
- **Voice recordings**—Allow kids to record their own voices repeating Bible verses and phrases.
- **QR codes**—This is a fun way for kids to find prepared answers using their own smartphones or devices.
- **Photo scavenger hunt**—Encourage kids to use phones or digital cameras to search for and document key information, hidden learning objects, or to find examples throughout the building.
- **Text answers to questions**—Invite older kids to text in their answers instead of raising their hands to answer. This can generate more honest engagement, especially on difficult topics.
- **Video calls**—Connect with absentees, missionaries, staff members, and other persons of interest as appropriate.

What about Marketing?

by Chuck Peters

Some people have a hard time reconciling the concepts of "ministry" and "marketing." At the surface level, the notion of marketing may bring about thoughts of selling or commercializing something. In reality, marketing might be better thought of as the communication of information about a product, event, or service that is of interest to a specific audience (or market) who has a need or desire to find the promoted item(s).

In the church world, marketing looks a lot more like an invitation, or series of invitations, to the gatherings that we host, rather than a commercial. Some of these gatherings may be special "big" events that only happen occasionally and have very large guest lists, but others may be smaller weekly gatherings for much smaller groups of people. In either case, the right people need to know the who, what, where, when, why, and how of each gathering so they are able to decide if they can or will attend, and who else they may wish to bring with them.

While marketing is an area of study that one could spend a lifetime learning and perfecting, here are a few foundational concepts to consider as you set out to market your ministry more effectively:

1. Demographics, Audience Awareness, and Segmentation: Know who you are trying to reach.

One of the most important things to do at the onset of any marketing campaign is identify who you are trying to reach. Professional marketers know that it is important to know who you are talking to, and that the wording, imagery, and means of communication you choose to use must all be tailored to the target audience. An advertisement for an event for young men age eighteen to twenty-four will use different pictures, words, colors, and fonts than an event for ladies age fifty-five and older. You may find that there are several sub-audiences or segments of an audience that merit distinct communication. For instance, it may be most effective to create multiple versions of an announcement for a church-wide family festival. One version may target young parents within the church who are regular attenders, another version may target recent visitors and newcomers to the church, and a third may address the general population of the church who are not young families. While the invitations may look similar in design, the specific messaging and call to action may change from, "bring your kids to fellowship with their friends," to "we'd like to get to know you better," to "come connect with young families in our church and community." Adjusting your message to multiple unique audiences makes your marketing more personal and appealing.

2. Impressions and Response Rates: Know what response to anticipate.

The goal of any marketing action is to generate a positive response. If marketing is an invitation, you want people to say yes to the invite. Marketers know, however, that expecting 100 percent of the people you invite to show up is not realistic. Principles of advertising tell us that people typically need to see something at least three times before they become aware of it. So it is important to run your advertisement for your new mid-week parents' group several weeks in advance of the first meeting, and to announce it in multiple places. You might consider printing it in the church bulletin, posting posters on hallway bulletin boards or in restrooms, and including the announcement in church-wide e-mails and through its social media channels. The more places a person sees the announcement, the more likely they will be to develop interest. These interactions with the ad are called *impressions*. More impressions generate more awareness and, thus, greater interest. All impressions are not created equally. Different types of impressions will generate different response rates. For instance, 5 percent of people who see an announcement for an event in the church bulletin or on a poster may decide to attend based on the ad. Ten percent may attend if the invitation is announced from the pulpit or in a classroom setting. But, 50 percent or more may decide to attend if they are subsequently invited personally by a leader. To reach a specific attendance goal for an event, you would do well to message more people than you want to attend (knowing that only a percentage of those messaged will respond), and to post the message in multiple places so that people will interact with the announcement at least three times.

3. Call to Action/RSVP Mechanism: Ask people to respond, and tell them how to do so.

Each ad or invitation should include a specific call to action that tells people how to respond. An announcement that merely says, "Family Festival, July 17th" is not as effective as one that says, "Join us for this year's Family Festival! Sign up in the foyer to reserve your space!" Give people a clear way to express interest or intent, and make it easy for them to do so. This serves you in a couple of important ways. First, it lets you get an idea of how many people to expect and prepare for at the event. Will you need hot dogs for fifty or two hundred fifty? It also gives you a list of prospects with which to follow up. Once someone has expressed interest by signing up, you can send them more detailed messages about the event. By signing up for the RSVP, they move a step deeper into your messaging, getting details on what to bring or how they might help. The foyer sign-up sheet is just one means of response. You might use a Google form, or Signup Genius. The point is to ask people to take a first-level action based on their interest.

4. Tracking and Analysis: Record what happens so you can adjust future strategy based on data.

The best way to gauge the effectiveness of your marketing efforts is to keep records of the actions you take and the response they generate. For instance, you can make an announcement from the pulpit inviting the whole congregation to sign up in the foyer and see how many do so as a result. Two days later you might make a post on social media that points people to a sign-up form and track how many respond through that channel. Test sending invitations with more detail and others with less detail. Test the use of printed ads, and test using video. In each case, record the results you generate and use the information you gather to hone future strategy. As you track the response generated by different types of marketing, you will gain valuable insight into how to best communicate with your intended audience.

5. Be Creative: Marketing is more effective when it is fun.

Marketing messaging is the most effective when it is communicated creatively. The first four principles listed here apply regardless of how creatively you name your events or advertise opportunities, but their effectiveness in generating interest can be increased exponentially when you deliver the information in creative, exciting, and memorable ways. Don't just announce a pizza party—have a delivery guy interrupt children's church to bring a special message inside a pizza box. Advertise your food drive by pushing an empty shopping cart onto the platform, then challenge the congregation to see how many carts they can fill. You can make your causes more compelling by making your marketing fun and creative.

Understanding a few marketing principles can help you immensely as you promote your ministry in the church and in your community. (They can also help you in your efforts to recruit volunteers to serve along with you.) Careful communication and creative messaging are great resources for promoting your ministry.

CHAPTER 4

DO I HAVE TO DO THIS ALONE?

DEVELOPING YOUR MINISTRY TEAM

Introduction

We've dressed it up and called it many different names. We work diligently to make it look inviting. We promise to do everything we can to make it easy. We even give in to using guilt and shame in an attempt to meet the need, yet we all still struggle with filling slots for preschool worship care.

Cindy and Myra saved my bacon. I was new. I was the first full-time Kids Minister and my responsibilities included all kids from birth to sixth grade. I was in way over my head, being pulled in multiple directions, and our extended session (preschool worship care) was screaming, "Help!" We found ourselves in a familiar place, more need than volunteers, and those SAINTS that were volunteering were getting tired and needing a break.

One night while lying in bed worrying about extended session, the Lord made it very clear to me, "You're not supposed to do this alone." I was both ecstatic and baffled. I was glad to hear this but didn't know what it meant. I didn't have a budget to hire anyone and I didn't really know anyone from which to ask help. That's when two best friends, Myra and Cindy, showed up. They had preschoolers in the program, noticed the problem, and believed they could help.

I was quick to thank them (I wanted to honor them with a parade through the city, but they thought that would be a little much . . .), relinquish the helms, and partner with these two ladies to organize and staff one of the most important ministries of our church.

I learned a valuable lesson. You do not have to do kids ministry alone. As a matter of fact, our job as ministry leaders is to equip, empower, and encourage. Praise God for Ephesians 4:12: "Equip the saints for the work of ministry, to build up the body of Christ." That verse and that situation changed my ministry.

What about Enlisting Volunteers?

by Bill Emeott and Jeremy Carroll

Regardless of the size of your church, everyone seems to need more workers. Just when you think you've finally filled all the vacancies, someone resigns. What do you do?

Kids ministry leaders share with me all the time about how frustrating and discouraging enlistment can be. Unfortunately, I don't have a "magic potion" that will guarantee you will discover and develop leaders, but I do think there are some good principles that will help us recruit well and retain those who join our team.

- **God is in control.** Pray! God wants your ministry to be a success! Start the enlistment process in prayer, asking God to lead you as you seek leaders and touch the hearts of those whom He desires to serve in your kids ministry. Philippians 4:19 teaches that God will supply all our needs. Why would He forget you when it comes to your need for leadership in the important work of kids ministry? Ask, seek, knock, and know that God is in control.

- **Know a good recruit when you see one.** Before you begin enlisting, know what you're looking for. Kids look up to their leaders. Make sure that those you recruit are people who will make strong, positive role models for boys and girls. Some characteristics of a good recruit include the following:
    - ❖ **A growing Christian:** Look for men and women who have a growing relationship with God.

❖ **An active church member:** Leaders of kids should be active, supportive members of your church.

❖ **Called by God:** Nothing can take the place of knowing you are called by God to lead kids. Seek folks who sense God is leading them to kids ministry.

❖ **Loves kids:** A no-brainer, right? Wrong. Unfortunately, not everyone who works with kids at church truly loves them. Many folks find themselves being persuaded by a plea or somehow guilted into ministry with little concern or true love for kids and their spiritual well-being. Watch to see those to whom kids naturally gravitate. You'll probably find a recruit who genuinely loves kids.

❖ **Willing to prepare:** I've not met a curriculum yet that prepares itself! There is a certain amount of preparation that is required whenever you lead kids. Be honest about the required preparation, and make sure your recruits are willing to devote time to this important aspect of kids ministry.

❖ **Willing to be a part of a team:** Kids ministry programming is never a solo act. You'll always need multiple leaders working together. Strive to recruit team players who are willing to work with the team to carry out the goal.

• **Organization is your friend.** Get organized. Know what you need and create a spreadsheet to help you see where you are and the progress you're making. I find it rewarding to "fill in the blanks" as God leads folks to volunteer. Know that staffing church ministries means you should always have at least two unrelated adults in a room with minor children (anyone under the age of eighteen). That rule should never be broken. Move toward a healthy teacher/child ratio in each classroom. A recommended ratio depends on the ages of the children.

- ❖ Babies—1:2 (1 adult for every 2 babies)
- ❖ 1s & 2s—1:3 (1 adult for every 3 kids)
- ❖ 3s & 4s—1:4 (1 adult for every 4 kids)
- ❖ Kindergarteners—1:5 (1 adult for every 5 kids)
- ❖ Grade School Kids—1:6 (1 adult for every 6 kids)

- **Use a ministry description.** When approaching a possible volunteer, be ready with a written job description. Not a six-page dissertation for which they'll need an attorney—but a simple half sheet of paper with five to six bullets describing what their job entails. Using a job/ministry description shows the value of the position for which you're recruiting. It says that you've thought about it and that it's important. It gives you something to hand a potential volunteer that they can read to make an honest decision. People fail to live up to our expectations because they don't know what we expect! Clearly stating the expectations up front will position both you and the recruit for success.

> People fail to live up to our expectations because they don't know what we expect!

- **Share the joy.** Jesus let His followers share in recruiting, so why wouldn't you (John 1:31–51)? You don't have to do all the enlistment yourself. Use current leadership to help you. As the ministry leader, concentrate on recruiting key leaders who will serve as directors over your major programs and events, and together recruit leaders who will serve under that director's leadership. When you approach recruiting in this way, everyone does a little. Together you've completed the task and you've "shared the joy!"

- **Recruit with a vision.** People want to be a part of something that is important. Know the reason for the program you're recruiting for and start there. If it's important, if it has an eternal purpose, if it is worth their effort, they're more likely to say yes. But if they're not aware of the *why*, it's easy to say no. Equally, no one wants to be part of something that's not exciting. Share enthusiastically the opportunity your church has to minister to young families. Vision, enthusiasm, and excitement are contagious!

- **Don't forget the men.** Don't assume that kids ministry is just for women. Men are great assets in a classroom. Remember that men are generally more open to organized, meaningful, and specific assignments. Be very intentional when recruiting guys.

- **Consider the "buddy system."** Some leadership roles can look a bit overwhelming. However, if two friends are recruited to fill a particular position as co-leaders, co-teachers, or co-directors/coordinators, the task can seem more doable. When recruiting two friends, it might even look fun! First-time volunteers will be more open to agreeing to serve with a buddy. Good friends are more apt to say yes when asked to serve together.

- **Train and equip your volunteers.** There's nothing more frustrating than being asked to do a job and then not being given the tools you need to do it well. Tell recruits that you'll provide them with the resources and training, explore different options (one-on-one over coffee, group training at church, electronically delivered training to their inbox, or provided through an online service), then do it!

> First-time volunteers will be more open to agreeing to serve with a buddy.

- **Support and appreciate your leaders.** Show your support by showing your face. A quick "drop-by" or a "peek-in" helps them know that you support them and are available if they need you. Everyone wants to feel appreciated, and usually it's the little things that mean the most. Quick notes or an e-mail; a candy gram with a short note of thanks attached; a "teacher of the week" profile on a ministry board; and yes, even the old pat on the back with a sincere thank-you can show your leadership team members how valuable they are and how much you appreciate them. A little affirmation mixed with a heaping dose of appreciation will go a long way in maintaining a volunteer ministry.

Recruitment of volunteers in children's ministry can sometimes feel like being stuck between the proverbial "rock and hard place." We want to make signing up to serve as easy as possible, but we also want to enlist the highest quality of volunteers possible—which often means volunteer applications, background and reference checks, and more. How do we make it simple without making it hard? The answer: **Have a repeatable process.**

Remember: **Relationships are key.** Often out of weariness, we resort to mailed cards, bulletin announcements, and mass e-mails. While these efforts may be slightly effective in spreading awareness, they will be less effective in actually enlisting new people. Even in a techno-digital age, people respond to relationship. If you have a committee or team for your ministry, ask them to recruit from the relationships they have as well. Remember that enthusiasm is contagious. When you personally share the joy of your ministry with others, it will catch on.

Never stop! Always be on the lookout. If your kids ministry is growing, you're never going to be finished recruiting and enlisting volunteers. Be watchful of whom God is bringing into your ministry and expect Him to provide all your needs "according to his riches in glory in Christ Jesus" (Phil. 4:19).

What about Building a Team?

by Klista Storts

You've come to the realization that you can't (and don't have to) do it alone. Now it's time to gather a team of people willing to come alongside and work with you to make your vision a reality. But whom do you ask to join you? The typical human response is to search for people just like us. Same personality. Same gifts. Same ideas. Same . . . same . . . same. Hmmm.

What if, by chance, you're not right? What if a situation needs something other than what you have to give? What if God gifted someone else differently for a reason? For a better and more balanced kids ministry, you need to welcome people on your team with various gifts, unique skills, and different personalities than you.

Chances are, you've taken a personality test in the past. These assessments can be helpful in finding out what your strengths are but are also valuable when identifying your weaknesses. As a quick review, below are characteristics of four types of personalities:

Strong and Steadfast

Pros
- Confident
- Assertive
- Decisive
- Quick decision-maker
- Get things done

Cons
- Often harsh
- Puts programs above people
- Does not like to be told what to do
- Does not like to be questioned
- Can be viewed as not a team player

Prim and Proper

Pros
- Organized
- Follows the rules
- Fair across the board

- Detailed
- Unwavering

Cons
- Can seem unfriendly or uncaring
- Puts policies above people
- Gets caught up in the details instead of the vision
- Not flexible
- Sometimes meticulous to a fault

Fun and Friendly

Pros
- Enjoyable to be around
- Lively
- Agreeable

Cons
- Sometimes hard to take seriously
- Can be impulsive
- Can appear to be careless

- Puts people above pro-
  grams and policies
- Spontaneous

- Often disorganized

- Forgets to focus on details

Agreeable and Adaptable

Pros
- Friendly
- Non-threatening
- Puts people over programs,
  policies, and self
- Responsive
- Compliant

Cons
- People-pleaser
- Lacks confidence
- Indecisive

- Can be viewed as weak

So, ouch! And, so what? The real takeaway on these may be in the "cons" section. Although you may have a favorable view of your leadership capabilities, those you lead unfortunately may sometimes view you on the negative side.

For example, if you are one of those "Strong and Steadfast" leaders, you may feel you are the most qualified leader ever. After all, you have great leadership characteristics! But people on your team may feel you're arrogant and hard to work with. That being said, as you look for team members, you might want to look for people on the "Fun and Friendly" or "Agreeable and Adaptable" side. You can ask their advice on how to handle difficult situations that require a bit more gentleness than you have.

If you're a people-pleasing "Agreeable and Adaptable" type, your team may be thinking, *Please! Just make a decision and stick with it!* This can be one of the most tiring leadership personalities because you are constantly changing with the tide around you so as not to upset anyone. That's a hard place to be. You need someone like a "Prim and

Proper" or "Strong and Steadfast" to help you stick to policies when you really need to—even if someone disagrees.

And "Fun and Friendly," although you truly may have a fantastic vision of what you want to see in the lives of kids, your team may not be able to see that in you. You need to show your serious side every now and then. It will boost the confidence level that your pastor, team, parents, and kids have in you. Ask for help in the details from "Prim and Proper." If you have a "Strong and Steadfast" on your team who seems to be wanting to push you out of the way, give her a project to lead! This will help her know she's needed and give her the respect she desires and deserves.

There is no right or wrong, better or worse personality. All have their ups and downs. The key is mixing the right ones together to get the perfect balance for your ministry. The good news is that knowing this opens your eyes to a whole new set of people to enlist for your team. Now, go out and mix it up!

> There is no right or wrong, better or worse personality.

What about Expectations?

by Shelly Harris

Volunteers need to have clear information about what to expect and what you expect of them. If you want to frustrate your volunteers, do not clearly communicate your expectations. People cannot meet expectations that they do not know about. Clearly communicating expectations will help everyone stay on the same page. It also allows you to hold a volunteer accountable should the need arise.

What should we expect from volunteers?

- **Be early.** Kids need to be greeted! Being early allows you to assess the room, gather supplies, and pray for your kids.

- **Follow your church's policies.** Complete your volunteer paperwork, including any background checks that the church needs to run. All volunteers should read the church's policy manual for kids ministry and follow those policies.

- **Teach God's Word.** Every age group should hear about God and the truths of His Word in an age-appropriate way. From simple playtime reminders that "God made you and loves you" in the baby room to detailed Bible stories and activities in the preteen room, kids should hear the truth of God's Word.

- **Be consistent.** Your church is relying on you. The kids in your group are relying on you. When you are unexpectedly absent, visitors and kids can worry. If you need to be absent, clearly communicate with your children's minister or area leader about how to arrange a substitute.

- **Continue to learn.** If your church offers training, go. If you find a book that will help you understand learning styles, read it. If you know a teacher is really effective, ask to observe his class. Seek opportunities to learn how to serve kids, parents, and families in your church and community.

How should you rotate schedules?

- Decide what type of rotation schedule works for your church. While rotation schedules may be needed, look for ways to create consistency. Is it possible for someone to serve once a month in the same class instead of different classes? Can you pair a rotation leader with a leader who teaches every week? The more consistency you can create, the more ownership and connection rotation volunteers will feel in your ministry. Ownership and connection are essential to retaining rotation volunteers.

- Remember that any rotation schedule requires more communication from you. People will need to be reminded that it is their turn to serve . . . every single time they serve.

- Many rotation volunteers are not as inclined to planning and preparation as your regular teachers are. Consider packing a box for rotation volunteers each week that contains everything they need to teach the suggested session.

- Pair a new rotation volunteer with an experienced volunteer, even if only for a short time period. Serving with someone who knows the kids, schedule, and room can calm nerves and help new volunteers learn the ropes.

- "Do I require parents or do I not require parents to serve?" Every church I have been a part of has had to answer this question. Some churches believe it is necessary to require parents to serve in the kids ministry. Other churches want people to serve where they feel called. There are pros and cons to both situations. Do you want to have more volunteers even if they aren't serving for the "right reasons"? Do you have parents who do not need to serve because of past or current life situations? Do you need more volunteers for safety reasons and you've exhausted other possibilities? Are you looking for helpers to support the regular leaders? Are you looking for leaders to teach the kids? Do you want a volunteer team that is passionate about kids ministry? Answering these questions will help you know whether you want to require or suggest parents serve in the kids ministry.

What if I need to "fire" a volunteer?

- Take time to evaluate the concern(s). Is this valid? Is this a miscommunication? Does the volunteer need to be fired, retrained, or reassigned? Can you pair a reliable leader with them to solve the problem? Is the safety of the kids in question? Is this a sin issue?
- You cannot avoid hard conversations. Ask another member of your ministry team to be a part of the conversation. You need a witness and someone to help reinforce what you are saying so your volunteer doesn't feel like you are against them personally. Be sure to keep your pastor informed.
- While conflict can be tough, seek to handle it with gentleness. Let the leader know you are thankful for their willingness to serve. Look for something good that they have done. Highlight it.
- If possible, try to find them a better fit. Sometimes, you cannot do this and the solution is simply a parting of ways. Other times, you find that someone who did

not click with preteens is a wonderful first grade teacher or greeter.

Your volunteer team is essential to your ministry. You cannot teach every class by yourself. You need volunteers. The kids in your ministry need to see a variety of people serving, each with their own unique set of gifts and abilities. Equip your volunteers to find joy in serving by clearly communicating expectations and addressing conflict graciously.

What about Training?

by Klista Storts

Training is an integral part of equipping your teachers, but with today's busy schedules, it can sometimes be one of the most challenging tasks to accomplish. Because your leaders have less and less time to give, be sure to honor that gift and make the best use of the opportunities entrusted to you.

Tell Them Your Vision

Leaders are more likely to commit to training when they recognize the importance of their service. You can help by communicating the vision for your kids ministry. Share your goals and your plans to achieve those goals. Once they understand the significance of their role, they will be more eager to prepare for it.

Resources

Just as a coach would never send a football player onto the field without the right equipment, you shouldn't send a teacher out without the essential materials he or she needs to be successful. Choose your curriculum with the end result in mind, and equip your teachers with the resources they need.

Employ various methods to guide your leaders in the use of the resources they have. Be creative. Don't just add another meeting to an already busy schedule. Take advantage of tools such as social media, blogs, video, and e-mail. Today's teachers will appreciate the ability to train at the times that are best for them.

Agenda

When you do need to schedule a meeting, be sure your teachers know the purpose. Make them aware of the agenda beforehand. In addition to the priorities on your list, ask your teachers what they need to talk about and what questions they have. When they know the *why*, they'll be more likely to attend.

Involve

Give your leaders ownership in the ministry. Involve them when planning meetings and encourage them to be a part of goal-setting. Take advantage of the skills of teachers. If someone is especially gifted in Bible storytelling, ask her to teach the others some of her best methods. Ask another to share great outreach and inreach ideas. Even the assignment of bringing snacks can be a reason for a teacher to commit to attend a meeting.

Nurture

The adage "people don't care how much you know until they know how much you care" rings true when working with your leaders. Make sure your volunteers know that you care about them—not just about what they can do for the ministry.

Many times, children's leaders have little adult interaction with other church members and can sometimes feel lost in the crowd. Offer times of devotion and inspiration. Do a book study together as a team. Interact outside the church. Take time to recharge and have fun. In essence, form a "small group" that can pray together, grow together, and support each other.

It's Worth It!

Ultimately everything you do to educate, encourage, and inspire your teachers will impact the lives of the kids and families in your ministry. So, while there may obstacles to overcome, the outcome will be worth the time and every effort you invest.

What about Paid Workers?

by Delanee Williams

Ideally, every kids ministry would be staffed with enough volunteers for all ministry programs and special events. But for some churches, the reality is that in certain circumstances, they must utilize employed teachers. The leadership you provide for volunteers and employed teachers is similar in many ways, but also differs in other ways. Keep in mind the points listed below as you interview, hire, train, and communicate with employed teachers.

Interviewing and Hiring

- Develop a written job description listing the position title, the determined qualifications, skills needed, and duties.

- Research and comply with local and federal guidelines for tax and employment issues.

- Follow your church's personnel procedures for hiring individuals. Additionally, adhere to your church's safety and security policies and procedures for all adults (volunteer or employed) serving with minors.

- Abide by the interview and hiring process for individuals established by your church.

- Develop a pay scale and structure. Keep in mind the position responsibilities, years of experience, and if the applicant has a degree beneficial to the position.

- Consider writing a policy manual specifically for employed teachers, including church personnel policies, the preschool and children's ministry policies, and other pertinent information.

Training

- Guide each new teacher through an orientation process. Include a tour of the church, specifically the area and environment applicable to the teacher. Remember to explain policies and procedures, including emergency evacuation routes. Providing a list of items to review is helpful to ensure the teacher is given a thorough orientation.

- Pair together beginning teachers with seasoned teachers to provide a mentoring relationship.

- Schedule ongoing trainings throughout the year. Plan various topics for the specific roles, levels of skills, and responsibilities of the teachers. Some examples may include: CPR/First Aid training, how to use the Bible with preschoolers and children, characteristics of children and how they learn, etc.
- Periodically highlight and review different policies and procedures from the employed teacher handbook.
- Check with your insurance company and local and state agencies for other ideas of possible training topics and material.
- Include team-building activities during training times to foster a feeling of community among the teachers.
- Provide opportunities for spiritual growth, like an occasional retreat or a workshop teaching the spiritual disciplines of prayer and Bible study.
- Remember to lead by example. You continually train teachers by your words and actions. Display how you want them to interact with others and fulfill the responsibilities.

Communication

- Communicate expectations to all teachers. Check for understanding, and hold them accountable.
- Schedule a time for formal feedback for each teacher. Many churches schedule evaluations once a year. For new teachers, consider scheduling an additional evaluation within the first year. Develop a written evaluation tool that correlates with the job expectations. Communicate what the teacher is doing well, how

the teacher can improve, and allow for feedback and questions from the employee.

- Provide ongoing and informal feedback to teachers. Feedback shouldn't be limited to the formal yearly evaluation.
- Affirm and encourage leaders verbally, by writing notes, and by sending birthday and thank-you cards.

Just as volunteers are vital to any ministry, employed teachers are as well. They have an opportunity to teach and minister to children and their families at church. As kids ministry leaders, we do our part in interviewing, hiring, training, and communicating so our employed teachers can effectively do their part in ministering to and teaching children and families.

CHAPTER 5

ARE ALL KIDS LIKE THIS?

UNDERSTANDING THE KIDS IN YOUR MINISTRY

Introduction

I have four nephews who were adopted into our family. All four were born in Taiwan, and I'm amazed at the questions their parents get from what I think are well-meaning people. The one that really floors me is, "Are they twins?"

No, they're not! They are eleven, ten, eight, and six years old—none of them are twins. Yes, they may look similar (or at least very different than their parents) but they are not twins (and, if you're counting, there's four of them).

Similarly, we sometimes might be guilty of not recognizing that all the kids in our ministries aren't the same. Each child is unique and (even if you really have twins in your ministry) has his or her own personality, likes and dislikes, preferences, strengths, and weaknesses. And it's our responsibility to minister to them all!

This chapter is dedicated to helping you understand the uniqueness of kids, recognizing that while each child has been created in God's image, each is a unique masterpiece of His creation. So we

celebrate, embrace, and minister to unique, individual children, sometimes as a group and sometimes individually.

What about Today's Kids?

---

by Jana Magruder

The truth about today's kids is that, generationally speaking, the verdict is not totally in. We are still watching how they will develop and mature into society. Known as Gen Z, there are some things that we already know for sure. Here are five traits that describe who you are seeing in your kids ministry:

1. They are a big part of the population. Born between 1996 and 2014, they make up 24.3 percent of the U.S. population, according to U.S. Census estimates for 2016. That's more than Millennials (22.1 percent), more than Gen X (19 percent), and more than Baby Boomers (22.9 percent).[7]

2. They are digital natives. Today's kids have never known a world without smartphones and tablets. Many of them have been actual users of devices since toddlerhood. Therefore, screens have been part of their development and have taken a disproportionate part of their development away from playing outside, reading books, and spending time with friends and family—in person.

3. They are being raised in a post-Christian society. Many kids in this generation are growing up in homes where there is no religion at all. They live in a secular world and the gospel, in many cases, has never been heard.

4. They are longing for acceptance. Because social media is such a dominant part of their lives *and* many of their parents' lives, kids today are longing for likes and positive comments on the pictures and stories they share on various social accounts. They are constantly aware of when they are not included because everything is documented in their classmates' digital lives.

5. They are anxious. Many studies show that this generation has higher anxiety rates than ever before. Because of the traits we just listed, it's no surprise that kids today suffer from anxiety and other psychological disorders.

So, what can the church do in light of these things? Our Kids Ministries are serving this generation described above, and while we don't know everything about them yet, we know enough to identify that we have an urgent need to display and teach the gospel to them—just as we have in every generation before. As leaders, we should not assume there is a strong foundation of biblical literacy or discipleship taking place at home. Praise God for the parents who are owning their role as primary disciplers, but the reality is that even our "church kids" often spend a disproportionate amount of time on screens and extra-curricular activities, rather than spending time in God's Word.

Research tells us that the typical church attender—in good standing with the church—attends only two to three times a month (as opposed to two to three times a week just twenty years ago).[8] This includes what you might consider your regular church attenders who are following Christ and seeking to live for Him. Therefore, train your volunteers to emphasize the gospel each week. Because the whole Bible is about Jesus (Luke 24), no matter what Bible story is being taught, we can always point back to what Jesus did for us on the cross. Spend the few hours you have with the kids in your ministry each month in the Bible, focusing on Bible skills, and encouraging kids to read their Bibles at home. In the book *Nothing Less*, I share about the number-one indicator of spiritual health in kids being Bible reading. This means that kids who read the Bible throughout childhood and adolescence have a much better chance of being spiritually healthy adults.

In conclusion, we should seek to be the kind of ministry where godly men and women are sharing about the love God has for each of us. This kind of love transcends the immediate gratification a typical Gen Z kid craves from his or her peers and how many "likes" they got for the day. We should seek to develop real relationships that have a positive influence on the kids in our trust and care. After all, many of the relationships in their lives are glazed over by the safety of a screen. Authentic and real conversations can help kids feel connected and ready to hear and respond to the gospel. Our heavenly Father is the only One who can fulfill the need for love and acceptance that kids today have—a love that a million followers or a zillion "likes" could never even come close to fulfilling. Let's strive to give them gospel love.

What about Differences?

by Jana Magruder

One of the biggest joys of leading children's ministries is the opportunity to serve all children. We are all made in God's image, so we delight in being able to welcome kids and families who may have learning or physical challenges, or who may even be bored and under-challenged. It's important to be ready for any child that walks through the door. Two big categories to prepare for are the following:

Be Ready to Serve a Variety of Special Needs

There are several ways to approach a special needs ministry. The important thing to champion is that not all children with special needs are served in the same way. Remember, parents who have a child with special needs need the church, and the church needs them. They have a higher risk of divorce, they have constant appointments with doctors and school counselors, and they more than likely have fewer friends and struggle to find Christian community. Because there is not one profile for children with special needs, it may seem overwhelming to accommodate everyone who has a need with appropriate measures.

Start with the following and commit to finding out more as you encounter and engage with families who need a strong children's ministry for their child.

- **Implement a "buddy" program:** This is perhaps the most common way of helping children with special needs. Kids who need buddies can vary widely in the reason why. They may need help listening and not distracting others, or they may need help doing an activity. A buddy can also help a child who is not normally in the traditional class develop relationships with their peers. Conversely, all the other kids have the opportunity to be a friend to a child they may not always have that chance to spend time with. Buddies also help teachers be able to focus on the lesson and activities.

> Parents who have a child with special needs need the church, and the church needs them.

- **Create a sensory room space:** A sensory room does not have to be a state-of-the art, multi-million-dollar facility (which is the first thing that comes to mind). The most important thing is to find a safe space for kids who need to leave their classroom for a while. They may need to leave because they are overwhelmed, tired, or just unable to participate in an activity. A sensory room should be quiet, have a variety of things to interact with, and two or more adults who monitor and facilitate time in the room. Ideas for items to place in a sensory room may include puzzles, mats for rolling and tumbling, large bouncing balls, or various sensory bins/stations.

- **Host a regular parents' night out for families with children with special needs:** This doesn't need a lot of explanation. Set aside regular time on the calendar to bring their children. Make sure your volunteer ratios and safety standards are in place. Plan for a variety of activities. A movie may work for some kids, games with lots of movement may work for others, while some may enjoy a quiet creating space. The goal is healthy marriages, families, and the opportunity to share the gospel with kids of all abilities and their families.

Challenge Kids Who Are Ready to Go Deeper

In every kids ministry, there will always be those who are ready to move to the next level. They answer all the questions, they know the books of the Bible, and they have memorized countless Bible verses. Praise God for these kids! But how do you keep them engaged? The last thing you want is for them to be bored, or worse—to be a distraction to other children. Here are a few things to keep in mind:

- **Give them a leadership role:** Find ways for them to share about what they've learned about a particular story. Encourage them to recite Scripture in front of their peers. Allow time for them to tell about interesting information that adds to the teaching time.
- **Challenge them with extra Scripture reading and memory:** If you already do a Bible reading challenge, give them a bonus to keep going. Reward appropriately.
- **Encourage them to share their testimony:** Some of these kids are ready to share their faith. What better

way for them to practice than to allow them time to share in class! This also allows other kids to have a model to watch in action.

As you can see, this is just the tip of the iceberg when it comes to serving a variety of children with multiple abilities. More than anything, we must remember that we are called to serve them all. That's why you're in this—to display the gospel to all of God's image-bearers!

What about Learning Preferences?

by Bill Emeott

"Train up a child in the way he should go: and when he is old he will not depart from it" (Prov. 22:6 kjv).

I've heard that Bible verse all my life. I memorized it early on, and my parents held tight to that verse as they worked diligently to "train us up" in church and with a biblical foundation. Several years ago, I began to read Proverbs 22:6 differently. As I considered the kids in my ministry and how they all seemed to have unique and specific "training" needs, Proverbs 22:6 took on new meaning.

If we want kids to remember what we're teaching, we need to teach them in the way God created them to learn—in the way "they should go." God created them—each and every one of them—uniquely and with unique preferences, including preferences for how they learn best. There are at least eight learning preferences, including:

Verbal: The verbal learner loves words and is sometimes called word smart. He likes to read them, say them, write them, and expresses himself best with them. Verbal learners prefer activities that use language to express ideas and interact with others. They enjoy poetry, keeping a journal, and can learn quite well from reading prepared material on specific subjects.

Logical: The logical learner loves order and is sometimes called number smart. She likes sorting, making lists, charting, and understanding the relationships between various objects. Logical learners prefer activities that allow them to use reasoning and logic to solve problems.

Visual: Visual learners love to see what they're learning and are sometimes called picture smart. They like to see things that will help reinforce what's being taught. Painting, pictures, graphs, and maps can help the visual learner see what's being taught. Visual learners prefer activities that allow them to express ideas through pictures.

Musical: Musical learners love anything to do with music and prefer activities that involve music and rhythm. Listening to, singing along with, tapping rhythmic patterns, or creating original tunes and lyrics will help reinforce Bible truths being taught.

Physical: The physical learner is sometimes called movement smart. She loves the "hands-on" experiences. She wants to touch things and prefers activities that require physical movement and coordination. Physical learners use their entire body to learn.

Natural: Natural learners love to investigate, examine, care for, and reflect on God's creation and are sometimes called nature smart. Natural learners learn best in and through encounters with the natural world.

Relational: Relational learners like being around, doing things with, and helping others. Relational learners are sometimes called people smart and enjoy being a part of a small group, on a team, and attending social gatherings. The relational learner works with and relates well to other people.

Reflective: Reflective learners are sometimes called self-smart and learn best through self-reflection. Reflective learners enjoy down time alone, may shy away from others, and have well-thought-out opinions.

Reflective learners prefer self-paced projects, independent quiet play, and can be highly intuitive.[9]

As leaders, we, too, will have a preferred learning approach and, if not intentional, will teach the way we prefer to learn. BE CAREFUL. As teachers, our goal should be to know and understand the kids we teach and build relationships with them so that we choose teaching methods that help to identify and cultivate a child's learning preference. Understanding the different approaches to learning and their implications takes the focus off the teacher and places it on the kids, where it needs to be.

> It's time to stop asking, "How smart is a child?" and start asking, "How is a child smart?"

Variety truly is the spice of life when it comes to teaching. Because every kid is unique and unique kids have unique preferences, teachers must strive to offer a variety of approaches each week as they lead kids to hear, study, and apply biblical content.

I think it's time to stop asking, "How smart is a child?" and start asking, "How is a child smart?" Kids are sitting in our churches waiting for someone to teach them in the way God created them to learn.

What about Teaching Methods?

by Rhonda VanCleave

You know that kids learn differently based on where they are developmentally. And, you know that each kid has a learning approach or two that are his "sweet spots." These approaches help things click in the brain and permeate the heart. But how do you hit those targets? What methods do you use? A bit of research reveals countless (really, you can't begin to count them!) lists of ideas. Even a "best of" list could be mind-boggling. The good news is that most reliable curricula will have done the legwork for you. As you read through the suggested activities, keep a few things in mind.

- **Be open to possibilities.** You will naturally gravitate toward methods that represent your own "sweet spot." When you choose those activities, they will feel natural to you and, more than likely, you will enjoy them. The kids in your group who share your affinities will enjoy them as well. However, as often as possible, also choose an activity that is your least favorite. Put on your game face and jump in there with a positive attitude. When you witness kids responding with interest and enthusiasm, you'll be glad you did.

- **Variety is key.** Even a short time of old-fashioned teacher-talking/kids-listening has a place when used in combination with methods that allow for movement, processing, and interaction. All kids have attention limits. Occasionally you'll find an activity that is so engaging that kids don't want to quit. However, it's a good idea to move to the next activity while the flame is still hot, rather than experiencing total burnout.

- **Structure helps.** Your regular sessions, regardless of the driving purpose (worship, Bible study, etc.), should follow a repeated structure. As kids follow a familiar path, they are primed to get the most out of any given method. Even within sections of a session, structure helps. For instance, in a large group time, kids may know to expect a reverent prayer or offering time, a lively praise time, an interactive Bible story, or a time when they will use their Bibles. However, variety can be implemented during those times. Prayer time might be a time of silent praying, or pop-corn prayers, or a responsive reading. The methods vary, but the structure helps provide stability.

Depending on the resource, most educational authorities identify three basic learning styles—Visual, Kinesthetic, and Auditory.

The good news is that many methods address more than one category. That's a win! For example, "highlighting information" is listed as a *visual* method. But it works as a *kinesthetic* activity if the child gets to mark on the paper or the poster (the bigger the better). It works for the *read and write* kids as they focus on the words. If the child reads the sentence aloud, you are engaging the *auditory* learner.

Almost all kids can learn from almost all methods, especially if they are motivated. If they have a great relationship with their teacher or their friends are engaged, kids can experience learning outside of their personal learning style. So, don't stress that some kids are "left out." If they are engaged, they will learn, and as you offer a variety of methods, you will hit their sweet spot too.

To get the ball rolling, here are some methods listed according to their primary learning style. (As you discover methods that really work for you, jot them down or keep a list to use when you need an alternative idea.)

Visual

Color-coding information	Showing or finding pictures or photos
Highlighting key facts or verses	Processing information using charts or graphs
Looking at maps	Engaging in art activities

Auditory

Participating in discussion

Listening to a story or monologue

Responding aloud

Explaining what you know

Reading aloud

Read and Write

Making lists

Copying words

Rewriting in "my own words"

Seeing or reading words

Using flash cards

Kinesthetic

Acting out a scene or using drama games

Participating in games that require movement

Building things

Making and using flash cards

Doing an activity (like tossing a ball) while learning

What about Guiding Behavior?

by Bill Emeott

When it comes to classroom management, I'd rather prevent a problem than deal with a problem. Over the years, this has become my mantra: Prevention is the preferred strategy! In other words, if it is at all possible to prevent a behavior issue, that's the route I'd prefer to take.

I believe that most children want to please the adults in their lives. However, we consistently hear that classroom management is one of the top three to four issues faced by kids ministry leaders today. In order to figure it out, I think we have to look at the root of the problem. Why is that student acting out? What would cause him or her to consistently misbehave?

Understanding the *why* behind misbehavior can help us know which systems to put in place that will allow kids to be successful, thus preventing poor behavior. This strategy takes time, effort, and energy . . . but it's worth it! Again, I'd rather work to prevent poor behavior than to deal with it.

Consider these *whys* of poor behavior:

For a variety of reasons, some kids **need more attention** than others and will do whatever it takes to get it. Work hard to give extra attention to this child. This will prevent outbursts and actions that fill his need in a negative way.

The class clown may be **masking her insecurity** and prefer to be laughed *with* than laughed *at*. Be careful not to create situations where this child chooses to hide his lack of knowledge (or maybe even his lack of ability to share his knowledge) by acting out. Remember, look past the actions and look for the cause.

Kids who haven't learned to **manage their anger** may need our help. Kids who "blow up" fast and are quick to "fight mode" may not have the skills to avoid these outbursts. Watch for opportunities to head off the poor behavior and give a child the chance to cool down and self-correct.

I was one of those kids who looked for **ways to be in control**. I wanted to be the teacher and would look for ways to fulfill my desire, even if it meant disrupting the teacher's plans. I often share with parents and teachers that the very thing that irritates you the most about your child, may be the very thing God wants to use for their success. I'm glad that there were understanding teachers in my past who saw past the

> The very thing that irritates you the most about your child, may be the very thing God wants to use for their success.

arrogance of my need for control and saw (and in some cases even chose to foster) my leadership potential.

Most kids I know are **full of energy**. It's the way God created them and part of His plan to help them develop. Unfortunately, many of us ignore that fact and spend week after week suppressing it instead of joining God in His plan. It's been said that children have an approximate one-minute attention span for every year they have been alive. Asking a four-year-old to sit still and listen for ten minutes goes against how she was created. Don't fight it—join it! Look for opportunities to include movement in your sessions. Get away from the tables and chairs and let the kids move!

When a child gets **bored** (or thinks he's bored), he starts looking for something to do. Most of the time it won't include the aim of the teacher. Some kids will get bored more easily than others, and you need to be ready for that. Plan sessions that consider the children, their preferences, and their abilities. More often than not, behavior issues can be connected to the sessions we plan (ouch).

Oftentimes kids don't live up to our expectations because they don't know what we expect. Make sure your **behavior expectations are understood**. Don't have a mile-long list of rules, but share that respect for each other is mandatory. That really clears out most of the issues. If you have kids who don't understand they are doing wrong, they won't know how to prevent that behavior/action.

At the end of the day, guiding behavior is all about knowing and understanding the kids you teach, then putting systems in place that will allow for success. Consider the why, then create a solution.

CHAPTER 6

WHAT IS GOD'S PLAN FOR KIDS?

SHARING THE GOSPEL IN YOUR MINISTRY

Introduction

Sometimes I sit and think about the kids in my life and I wonder what they'll be when they grow up. What will they choose to do with their lives?

Drake is very smart but kind of quiet; he'll make a good accountant. Fisher loves puzzles and figuring out how things work; he'll make a great engineer. Arthur is kind to everyone. He sees the best in every situation. I think he'd be a great middle school counselor. And, Jackson . . . it's still early, but I think he'll be a veterinarian. Jackson loves cats.

I really can't know God's plan for kids when it comes to choosing their life's profession. But I do know this: God wants every child to trust Jesus Christ and spend eternity with Him. And if I know this (and I do), then sharing His good news should be at the very core of everything I do.

Kids ministry is about sharing the gospel. We use a variety of ways, programs, events, and opportunities to do it, but that's the goal, that's the mark, that's the measure of our success. I hope you already know this, and I hope this chapter helps equip you to make sharing the gospel the cornerstone of your ministry.

What about the Age of Accountability?

by Bill Emeott

When can a child make a decision to become a Christian? This question haunts every Christian parent at some point, and oftentimes the question is quickly directed to you, the kids ministry leader. Unfortunately, it's not an easy question to answer.

What age a child can make a profession of faith is not answered with a number or a school year. The "age of accountability" is not even a biblical term. You won't find the phrase anywhere in Scripture. So we are challenged to approach the question with what we do know.

We do know that very young children are concrete in their thinking, and the idea of eternal salvation is very abstract. Therefore, we know that most young children will not be mentally and emotionally ready to understand the gospel. So, we look for maturity and genuine understanding.

We do know that most eight- and nine-year-old children are beginning to recognize the difference between fantasy and reality. Santa, the Easter Bunny, the Tooth Fairy, and even superheroes on cartoons are beginning to be seen for what they really are: fantastical, fictional, fun, and make-believe games. So, we look for maturity and genuine understanding.

We do know that there's not one way for an adult to receive eternal salvation and another for a child. Therefore, we can conclude that before a child can receive Christ as Lord and Savior, that child will need to have (at least in part) the ability to understand the basic concepts of sin and the gospel. So, we look for maturity and genuine understanding.

We do know that before a person can be saved, he must understand his need for a Savior. He must know what sin is, that he has sinned, that his sin is against God, and that his sin separates him from God. He must recognize his need for a Savior. So, we look for maturity and genuine understanding.

We do know that a person must be able to deal with (both mentally and emotionally) the basic truths of the gospel. She will need an appropriate understanding that Jesus came from God, was killed by man (according to God's plan), and rose from the dead, and she will need to sense in her heart the need to receive what God through Christ has done for her (through the work of the Holy Spirit). So, we look for maturity and genuine understanding.

There are some great Christian men and women whose testimony is that they made the decision to follow Christ at a very early age, and their salvation is obvious and is seen through their fruit. God can save anybody He wants to, and there is no specific age at which some magical accountability happens.

> Each child's journey is unique and should be handled individually.

But I do believe that very young children coming to a sincere mature and genuine understanding is unique. Therefore, we proceed carefully. We spend a lot of time with the child. We ask lots of questions, and we prayerfully discern—not emphatically prohibit—a child's desire to follow Christ.

Remember, a child's decision to follow Christ is often a journey, not just an overnight sleepover. Pray! Pray for God to discern for you a child's readiness. Pray that God will clearly reveal Himself to the child, and the child will clearly understand. Pray that each child you counsel will understand the gospel and know God's love and provision for sin through the free gift of Jesus. Pray that they will respond in confidence and receive forgiveness, salvation, and life with Christ for eternity. Rest in the knowledge that the gospel call will come to that child, giving him or her an opportunity to respond.

What about Sharing the Gospel with Kids?

by Karen Jones

Kids being transformed by the power of the gospel is what kids ministry is all about! It's the whole reason we do what we do! Knowing that, I think we can all agree that sharing the gospel with children is the most important thing we do. We should take care to handle it wisely.

Make Sure Kids Hear the Gospel Over and Over Again

Don't let the only time kids hear the gospel be in a formal "presentation" on Easter Sunday or at VBS. All of our teaching week in and week out should point kids to Christ's work on the cross. The gospel story is weaved throughout the entire Bible, so the gospel should be weaved throughout our entire ministry.

Involve Parents

Remember that God has ordained that parents are a child's primary spiritual leader. Any chance we have to involve parents in the process, we should. Talk with a parent about how to share the gospel with their child. Offer a class on evangelizing children for parents. Tell parents when you see God at work in their child's life. Rather than leading a child to pray to receive Christ on your own, encourage a child's parent to lead them.

Talk One-on-One

In large settings like VBS or a Fall Festival, we may be tempted to ask kids to raise their hands to make a decision or repeat a prayer after us. This is not a wise practice. God deals with each of us as individuals, and each child deserves one-on-one counseling. Talking with a child one-on-one will help you discern if the child really is under conviction of sin, if they understand what Jesus did to pay for their sin, or if they are feeling pressured to make a decision.

Use Tools

Really the only tool you *need* to share the gospel with a child is a Bible, but there are many helpful supplemental tools out there. I like *The Gospel: God's Plan for Me.* This resource walks you through sharing the gospel using kid-friendly words and points you to Bible verses to read together. Whatever supplemental tool you use, make sure it centers on the gospel, putting the emphasis on God and what He has done through Jesus, versus what we need to do.

Avoid Using Figurative and Symbolic Language

Remember you are talking to concrete thinkers. Avoid using churchy words or symbolic language like "ask Jesus into your heart," "make Jesus the Lord of your life," or "knocking on the door of your heart." Use words kids can understand like "trust in Jesus," "trust Jesus to be the boss of your life," or "Jesus is working in your life."

Listen More than Talk

Keep it conversational. Ask open-ended questions. Encourage a child to express her own ideas. Give time for the child to reflect and answer without giving her the answer. If the child can't answer within a reasonable time, consider rephrasing the question. Avoid giving more information than a child asks or needs.

Look for Evidence of Conviction

Unfortunately, many people who are living lives far from God think their eternity is secure because they prayed a prayer as a child. We need to carefully steward these little hearts God has put under our care. Look for signs of conviction of sin. Does the child understand he is a sinner? Can he tell you about sins with which he struggles? (Assure him he will not get in trouble for sharing.) When explaining how one becomes a Christian, does he use "good works" answers such as going to church, reading the Bible, getting baptized, praying, being good? (Emphasize that it is not these "good works" that make someone a Christian.)

Allow Children to Pray in Their Own Words

Encourage children to talk to God in their own words. Invite them to do so silently if they do not feel comfortable praying aloud. God knows what is going on in that child's heart. They may not get all the language right yet, but we can trust that the Spirit is interceding for them if God is truly working in their hearts.

Never Pressure a Child

We know many adults who have dramatic conversion stories, but most of the time, a child coming to Christ is a process. Don't mistake curiosity for conviction. It may take months or years of asking questions and putting the pieces together before God definitively calls a child to a point of decision. Be patient. Remember that God saves people, not us. By nature, most children want to please, so be sure you are not inadvertently pressuring them to "pray a prayer" by your zealousness for them to follow Christ.

Never Discourage a Child

Even if you discern that a child has not yet placed their trust in Jesus, affirm them and share their excitement that God is at work in their lives. Encourage them to keep asking questions and learning more and more.

Don't Rush Baptism

Take time to observe evidence that a child has truly turned from sin and trusted in Jesus before encouraging him to be baptized. Does the child have a new affection for Jesus? Is he quick to repent when he sins? Does he have a desire for spiritual practices like prayer and Bible reading? Does he show an increasing love for others? Moving slowly toward baptism does not mean that a child has not been converted. Slowness allows the parent and others to see the Spirit's work in the child. Furthermore, children may mistakenly identify the concrete act of baptism as a salvation experience. We want them to know the moment they turned from sin to Jesus is the moment they entered God's kingdom.

What about a Child's Response to the Gospel?

---

by Debbie Ruth

Mark 10 tells about a time when people brought their children to Jesus. What a beautiful picture of how Jesus receives children! Pastors and kids ministry leaders alike can apply important truths from this story to response times.

Jesus didn't stop the children from coming to Him. Can you imagine how glad Jesus was to see the kids? He knew each one of them by name!

- Express your delight that a child has come forward. Get on her eye level and focus your attention directly on her.
- Ask the child a leading question, such as, "Why have you come forward?"
- Quickly determine the child's comfort level. Many kids will express excitement, while others may be timid or even anxious. Explain that you (or a kids leader) would like to talk with her.
- Pray a short prayer thanking God for leading the child to come forward and for His plan for her life.

Jesus took the children in His arms. He showed compassion and gave them what they needed.

- Kids need time to process things. Escort the child and his parents or another adult to a quiet, yet public, place to talk. If you cannot do this yourself, involve a kids leader who is trained in sharing the gospel with kids.
- Listen! Ask simple questions to gauge his understanding, and don't assume anything. Avoid putting words in the child's mouth by helping him tell you what he is experiencing.
- Correct misconceptions and avoid using abstract language. Phrases such as "asking Jesus into your heart" and "wash away your sins" can be confusing to kids.
- Recognize that each child will be at a different point in his journey to salvation.

- Perhaps the child senses the Holy Spirit's leading and is beginning to ask questions. This child might need time to grow and learn. Encourage the child's involvement at church. Talk to parents about guiding conversation at home by asking questions such as, "What would Jesus want us to do?" or "What does the Bible say about . . . ?"

- It's possible that the child has a conviction of sin, but doesn't understand Jesus' saving act on the cross. Be ready to explain gaps in the child's understanding.

- Maybe a child feels a conviction of sin, understands Jesus' saving act through His death and resurrection, and is ready to trust Him as Savior and confess Him as Lord. This child already may have trusted in Jesus as his Savior, or he might be ready to do so now. Be ready to guide the child in taking the next step.

- Perhaps the child is making a decision at a time when parents are unavailable, such as at kids worship, Vacation Bible School, or children's camp.

  ❖ Christian parents likely will have prayed for this time in their child's life and be excited that their child is taking a step toward a relationship with Jesus. Inform the parents of the child's decision and schedule a time to visit together.

- Non-Christian parents may have questions or be unsure about their child's decision. Schedule a visit with the child and his parents. Assist the child in explaining his decision and be prepared to share with parents how they can trust Jesus as Savior.

Jesus blessed the children. Wouldn't we have loved to see Jesus bless the children? His transparency and theirs must have been incredible to watch!

- Be genuine as you talk with the child and her parents. Relax and lean on the Lord to guide you.
- Resist the desire to push the child. Many children need several conversations before they are ready to make a decision for Christ. Set up times to talk further with the child and her parents.
- Pray and rejoice with the child!
- Give the child a salvation booklet or devotional and a highlighter and assign her homework. Encourage the child to read the booklet with her parents and highlight verses in the Bible that explain God's plan of salvation. This will reinforce what you've talked about and make it easy for the child to look back at the verses.
- Encourage her to follow God's plan throughout her life! Involve the child in a new Christians' class or other kids' discipleship programs.

What about Discipleship?

by Kayla Stevens and William Summey

As kids ministry leaders, we champion discipleship. Our hearts long to see kids receive salvation, grow deeply in Jesus, and lead others to Him. It is why we do what we do!

The steps we take to disciple kids matter. While every context and church culture are different, there are key elements of discipling kids that are both biblical and valuable in helping us to catalyze our ministries. We can create opportunities for kids to hear the gospel, learn foundational truths, and practice what they learn.

Begin with the End in Mind

I learned early on in my ministry that the borders of my vision for kids ministry required me to have a generational telescope. As leaders we must look beyond the lines of student ministry or college graduation. Our target for kids' discipleship must reach to future generations who continue to make disciples.

Therefore, we begin with the end in mind. The discipleship practices we implement must be reproducible. Discipleship cannot depend on us alone. We want it to outlive us. The way we disciple kids needs be flexible and adaptable so they can understand, practice, and disciple other kids.

Make the Gospel Central

The gospel is what changes and transforms. It must permeate everything we do, including discipleship. We must be strategic to saturate each lesson and activity with the gospel. We sometimes make the mistake of thinking the gospel is needed in evangelism, but not in discipleship; but it is the gospel that we need most throughout every stage of our walk with Christ. Guide kids to recognize connections in each lesson to the big picture of God's story. Don't allow them to receive anything less than the whole counsel of God. Capture their hearts with the hope of the gospel now, anchoring their souls to His steadfast love for the journey ahead.

Identify Biblical Handles

Pinpoint truth handles for kids to grasp at various learning levels. Repeat them consistently and often. LifeWay's Levels of Biblical Learning® and Bible Skills for Kids are two of the most helpful tools I've found to help me chart the spiritual development of a child's understanding of key doctrines of the faith. They not only teach the depth of knowledge but do so across the growth chart from birth to the preteen years in words and concepts that they can understand best. Utilize tools like these to provide concise, measurable handles of discipleship. As they grow, kids learn to grasp the next level of biblical truth with the same anticipation of a sweaty seven-year-old reaching for the next rung on the monkey bars.

Levels of Biblical Learning

As kids grow, their understanding of foundational truths grows with them. For example, how does a twelve-year-old grow to learn the truth that "People can live with joy regardless of their circumstances"? It begins with teaching the truth as a baby that "God loves me." Notice how the concepts build upon the other as a child grows.

Younger Preschoolers can learn that God loves them.

Middle Preschoolers can learn that God will always love them.

Older Preschoolers can learn that no matter what happens, God loves people.

Younger Kids can learn that good and bad happen to people, but God still loves them.

Middle Kids can learn that people can respond in positive ways to what happens to them.

Preteens can learn that people can live with joy regardless of their circumstances.

Each concept is part of a deeper foundation laid even as the child is a baby and, with each passing year, a child's ability to understand more about who God is increases. Kids take each year of learning and build upon that to reach a greater understanding of how much God loves them.

Bible Skills for Kids

Bible Skills for Kids was developed by LifeWay Kids to provide teachers, parents, and ministers of preschoolers and children with Bible skill milestones. You'll find a sixteen-page booklet on how to teach Bible skills to kids, a poster with the milestones by age group, and free training videos.[10] Bible Skills for Kids covers nineteen Bible skills and concepts that preschoolers and kids can learn as they interact with and learn about the Bible from birth to the preteen years. Much like Levels of Biblical Learning, these skills and concepts progress and build upon previous skills and concepts to the goal of where kids can be at the end of the preteen years.

For example, children can learn these Bible concepts about the Bible's reliability:

Younger Preschoolers can hear the Bible is a special book.

Older Preschoolers can know that everything in the Bible is true.

Younger Kids can learn that Bible truths never change.

Older Kids can understand the truths in the Bible are without error and will last forever.

Open the Bible

Many tools are helpful in discipleship, but only one is essential. As we lead kids, we need to engage their hands and their hearts with the Bible. Our words falter. His endure. Encourage little fingers to touch the story in your Bible as you teach. Pair older and younger kids together to find Bible passages during large group time. Engage kids with their Bibles in age-appropriate ways, but make sure to engage them.

The 2017 LifeWay Research published in the book *Nothing Less* by Jana Magruder shows that Bible reading is the most important thing parents can lead their children to do to impact their spiritual health. Create space in your discipleship plan for kids to practice what they learn. Discipleship grows from the foundation of a lifelong connection to the Word.

Cultivate Relationship

As leaders, we have to develop relationships with our kids that communicate we care about their hearts, not just their attendance. Make the time to meet kids where they are, on the ball field, at their school play, or even in their homes. Discipleship flourishes in healthy, continuous relationships with both kids and their families. It requires trust, vulnerability, authenticity, and time. If kids can't see our hearts, they will never trust our words.

Prepare Effectively

There will always be valuable pieces of your ministry that require your attention. However, don't let what is helpful distract from what is essential. The Word is essential. Communicating truth consistently is essential. Discipline yourself to make room in your calendar to prepare well for the task God has called you to. Hold it as sacred. Don't allow supporting assignments to distract from the mission.

Pray Fervently

As you lead kids, remember that "unless the LORD builds a house, its builders labor over it in vain" (Ps. 127:1). Our battle for the hearts of kids begins on our knees. Be strategic and intentional about the time you spend in prayer for your kids and families. Keep a prayer journal. Make daily reminders on your phone. Pray out loud over your kids in those early prep hours of Sunday mornings. Leverage your time and your calendar to fight for the hearts and minds of your kids to be captured by King Jesus.

Discipleship is neither easy nor simple. It's messy. It's challenging and it's costly. And yet, this beautiful messy task is what God calls us to cultivate in the hearts and minds of kids in our ministries. It is our privilege and blessing to be a part of this work. They will one day take our place as disciple-makers. Let us commit to leverage our time, our abilities, and our resources for a greater vision of God-honoring multiplication of disciples.

What about Sharing Their Faith?

by Rhonda VanCleave

Can I be honest with you for a minute? I'm a pastor's wife, I lead the kids ministry at our church, I've developed curriculum, and I love spending time studying the Bible. But I still get weak in the knees when I think about witnessing to someone. It's a little easier if they ask me a question first. But my spiritual gift is NOT evangelism. While that doesn't give me a pass on sharing the gospel (the Great Commission applies to all of us), it does mean that it can really feel outside my comfort zone. So then, if you have similar feelings, how in the world do we help kids share their faith?

It may help to remember that the same Spirit that endowed you with your spiritual gifts also gives gifts to everyone (including kids) who trusts Jesus as Savior. So, you will find that some kids are truly like Philip and Andrew in the Bible who brought friends to Jesus (John 1:40–45). Encourage those kids! Help them realize that they are honoring God with their effort (which may seem effortless to them—that's the nature of a spiritual gift).

Then there will be kids who are not as comfortable. They need the same kind of "training wheels" that many of us "hesitant witnesses" need. Help them learn and practice the following:

1. **Know your own testimony.** Write it down. Practice sharing it with another believer whom you are comfortable talking with. Keep it short. A good rule of thumb is six to ten sentences or less than two minutes. The bottom line is, when it's your story, you are telling your own experience. That's hard to argue with.

2. **Know three or four Bible verses that help explain the gospel.** Choose verses that help explain clearly about becoming a Christian. Memorize them, or at least memorize the reference, and know that you can find the verses easily.

3. **Trust God's Holy Spirit.** Believe God's promise to give you the words to say when you need them (Luke 12:12). Even if you feel weak in the knees or have a tummy full of butterflies, know that if the Spirit nudges you to speak up, He will help you.

As you help kids prepare to share their faith with others, you will discover several bonuses. The confidence you help a child develop during the early years can more easily carry into adulthood. Processing their testimony helps to cement their own memory, thus putting up a defense against doubts that inevitably come. Practicing sharing their testimonies in comfortable settings helps kids be prepared when given an opportunity outside the walls of the church.

Whether it's Sunday school, weekday events, VBS, or a host of other church-related events, your best outreach are the kids (and leaders) in your own kids ministry. Encourage those kids who seem to easily encourage other kids to come. But also encourage those who are more hesitant. Encourage them each time they have a successful experience talking to a friend about Jesus or inviting a friend to church (and remember—the success is in the talking and inviting, not in the friend responding positively!), and they will be motivated to do it again. One great resource for guiding kids in sharing their faith is LifeWay's "Leading a Friend to Christ" tract.

> Equipping your kids to share the gospel and invite their friends is a part of your role as a kids ministry leader.

You can print flyers by the thousands, but it is the hands that deliver those flyers that make the personal contact. Equipping your kids to share the gospel and invite their friends is a part of your role as a kids ministry leader. And the effort is SO worth it!

CHAPTER 7

WAIT! I MINISTER TO FAMILIES TOO?

CONNECTING YOUR MINISTRY WITH FAMILIES

Introduction

If you really want to influence a child's life, influence her family.

I felt inadequate. I didn't think I had the skills or the expertise. I hadn't raised kids of my own, so how could I offer any credible advice? So I, for the most part, ignored the parents. Oh, I wanted them to serve, and I certainly wanted them to bring their kids (on time). I definitely wanted them to support me, but I never saw them as part of my kids ministry, and I should have.

If I could go back and do it all over again, there are certainly things I'd do differently. Perhaps on the top of that list is including parents as an important part of my kids ministry. Parents have more influence over their kids than I ever will. Of the 168-hour week, we see kids at church maybe 3 to 4 hours (at most!). Our influence is limited, but family influence is endless. Dedicate time and energy to influencing the influencers.

In the next several pages, we hope to help you see just how important families are to your success as a kids ministry leader. We hope you'll see your role as an encourager, equipper, and champion for the most influential people in a child's life—his family!

What about Today's Families?

by Jana Magruder

I am part of Generation X. We are a small generation compared to our parents (Boomers) and our younger siblings and friends, the Millennials. Gen X is known for being the "slacker generation" in our youth and over-achiever, helicopter parents as we aged up. Now, I am no sociologist, but I find it fascinating to look at all the generations, how we do life together, and how we are bringing up the next generation—Gen Z (also known as the iGeneration, for obvious reasons). These are the children represented in our kids and student ministries. The story is still out on this generation as experts watch how they emerge into adulthood (the oldest ones are in college). What we do know is that this generation has always been "on," never knowing a time where there were no computers, or for the younger ones in kids ministry, smartphones and tablets. Because of this, research is pointing to all kinds of things such as higher anxiety, less social skills, and less quality time with friends, family, and relationships in general. This translates to less time in our churches.

Research tells us that people are attending church far less than they did twenty years ago. A regular church attender twenty years ago attended three times a week. Now regular church attendees come to church three times a month (and sometimes less than that).[11] Families are no exception to this and have busy calendars scheduled with a variety of activities—many of them scheduled during church activities. Knowing this, our role as kids ministry leaders is to equip the parents to disciple their children at home. Of course, this should not be anything new—the Bible tells us that parents are to be the primary disciplers of their children. We cannot ignore Deuteronomy 6. However, because we see kids less than we used to, parents cannot depend solely on the children's ministry to disciple their kids for them.

This is tricky because we live in an outsourced culture. Many of us are used to outsourcing just about anything, especially when it comes to bringing up our children. If we want our kids to learn an instrument, we get them lessons. If we want our kids to improve at their sport of choice, we hire a personal coach. If they are struggling in school, we hire a tutor. You get the picture. While there is nothing wrong with getting kids extra help, it's concerning to realize that many parents are "outsourcing" the discipleship of their children 100 percent to the church.

To be clear, I absolutely rely on a math tutor to help my child with high school algebra. But as her mother, I cannot deny that God commands with the following: "Love the LORD your God with all your heart, with all your soul, and with all your strength. These words that I am giving you today are to be in your heart. Repeat them to your children. Talk about them when you sit in your house and when you walk along the road, when you lie down and when you get up" (Deut. 6:5–7). This command is for my husband and me to follow as we bring up our three children in life and faith.

When done best, the partnership between parents and their local church can be extremely beneficial shaping times of Bible study and worship for kids, as well as fun and exciting events that help parents and kids have experiences that allow more engaging conversations to continue at home. Kids ministry leaders can help equip parents with resources for at-home discipleship.

So, you may be wondering, *What about kids who don't have spiritually healthy parents to disciple them at home?* Good question. We all know kids in our ministries who fall into this category. The absolute best thing the church can do for these kids is to show up and serve regularly in children's ministry. Research tells us that when a child connects with several adults in their church who intentionally pour into them, they are more likely to be spiritually healthy when they become adults.[12] Godly men and women need to be speaking truth into the lives of these kids while developing a trusted relationship that shows this child that they care. Our churches must champion this effort. Our kids are worth it.

What about my Credibility and Authority?

by Karen Jones

I was twenty-seven years old when I was called to my first full-time position as minister to preschool and children. I was not married. I had no children. I had a seminary degree and a few years of teaching preschoolers and children under my belt, but I struggled with confidence in my new position. I understood the great responsibility God had entrusted to me, which was a good thing, but I was paralyzed with fear. Would people really take me seriously? How was I supposed to lead all those volunteers, most of whom were older than me? Did I have any business telling parents how to disciple their kids without any of my own? Here are some of the things I would tell my twenty-seven-year-old self now.

Trust God's Calling

God has placed you in this position. You are there by His sovereign design. God's very own Spirit dwells within you. God does not call the qualified; He qualifies the called. God put you in your position for a reason, and He will empower you to carry it out!

Give God Your Weakness

You will make mistakes in your ministry, probably many of them. It won't be the end of the world. I promise. In fact, our Father loves to show Himself in our weakness (2 Cor. 12:9). Some of your best days in ministry will be those where you feel like everything is falling apart. The Lord will surprise you in how He moves on those days. Staying low before the Lord is a great place to live!

Lean on the Authority of God's Word

Everything we do in our ministry to children and families should ultimately find its root in God's Word. Do not feel like you have to defend your ministry to naysayers based on your own authority or experience. Take them to the Bible.

Be Humble and Teachable

If you are single, understand that you really do not know what it is like to be married. If you do not have children, understand that you really do not know what it is like to be a parent. You will find there are people in your church that are better administrators than you. There are people in your church that know more about child development than you. There are people in your church who really could do your job much better than you! That is okay. Be humble. Seek out those people and learn from them.

Always Be Learning

There is no shortage of blog posts, books, conferences, and podcasts to equip kids ministry leaders. Read them. Attend them. Listen to them. Implement some of the things you learn. Talk to other kids ministry leaders in your area or various networks. Learn what they are doing. What works and what doesn't. I have always found other kids ministry leaders to be my best resources.

Find a Mentor

Something that really helped me when I was a newbie to ministry was finding a mentor. Identify someone in your same position at another church. Plan times to FaceTime or meet up for lunch. Just talking through ideas and struggles with someone who has been there makes a huge difference.

Get Your Hands Dirty

Delegation is absolutely essential in kids ministry. There is just too much for any one person to do on his or her own. Delegate, but be willing to get down and dirty when it is called for. Never ask anyone to do something that you are not willing to do yourself. Sometimes this means cleaning out the church van in 90-degree heat after a week at camp. Sometimes that means consoling the baby who cries for a solid ten minutes every time they are dropped off. Sometimes that means staying late on a Sunday until that last chatty parent finally picks up all their kids. Working hard on behalf of your kids and families will not go unnoticed.

Do What You Say You Will Do

You will easily undermine any credibility you have built by not following through with what you say you will do. Purchase that new toy you told your preschool teachers you would get for their room. Send out that weekly parent e-mail you committed to send. Set up a coffee date with that mom like you said you would. Show people that you are a person of your word.

The bottom line is: building credibility and authority with those to whom you minister takes time. Once people get to know you and what you are about, the respect will come. Trust the Lord. Rely on His power. Do your best. Love the kids and families God has entrusted to you. And watch God work in their lives . . . and yours too!

What about Deuteronomy 6?

by Rachel Coe

The Deuteronomy Partnership

Partner—a person who takes part in an undertaking with another or others, especially in a business or company with shared risks and profits.[13]

Kids leaders are partners with parents. Together you share the responsibility of teaching and guiding preschoolers and children in discovering biblical truths and applying them to life. It takes home and church working together.

Deuteronomy 6:4–9 clarifies the importance of teaching and guiding children in the truth of God's Word.

> "Listen, Israel: The LORD our God, the LORD is one. Love the LORD your God with all your heart, with all your soul, and with all your strength. These words that I am giving you today are to be in your heart. Repeat them to your children. Talk about them when you sit in your house and when you walk along the road, when you lie down and when you get up. Bind

them as a sign on your hand and let them be a symbol on your forehead. Write them on the doorposts of your house and on your city gates."

God assigned parents the primary responsibility for teaching and guiding children in the truth of God's Word. It is God's plan for families to begin the process of laying the foundations in children's lives. Families, however, can be supported in this remarkable role by the kids ministry leader.

1. What is the undertaking? Listen, follow, and teach all of God's statutes and commands.

Clearly, the goal is to lay foundations of faith, teach the Bible, model godly behavior and attitudes, share the good news of salvation, and encourage young believers to know what it means to be a Christ-follower.

2. With whom is the partnership? Both kids leaders and parents share in establishing and undergirding foundations of faith.

Assure parents of your desire to equip and support them as the spiritual leaders in their home. Motivate and encourage parents in your partnership with them by casting a vision. Help families see through your combined efforts the horizon of blessings ahead as their children delve into the Bible, hear about God and His Son, learn what it means to obey His statutes and commands, and grow to love others as Jesus loves.

> Both kids leaders and parents share in establishing and undergirding foundations of faith.

3. What are the risks? Whatever the risks, they are worth it.

Serving kids and families requires a heart for children and their needs. It also calls for patience, endurance, and focus. Kids leaders often face resistance and criticism of decisions and actions. On the other hand, kids leaders experience extreme joy and fulfillment through words of encouragement and support.

At the outset of your ministry, talk with parents about your goals and dreams for the kids ministry at your church. Ask parents for their input on programs, events, and even approaches for nurturing spiritual growth. Enlist the help of parents to teach, support, and pray.

4. What are the profits? When kids leaders and families work together, much can be accomplished.

Not only will families be confident and comfortable with what their children are experiencing at church, they will be your champions. Satisfied parents will encourage new families and visiting families to trust you and your church to guide and teach their children.

Children will be the greatest benefactors of hand-in-hand ministry between their families and church. Boys and girls will sense and appreciate the strong connection between home and church. Kids will be excited and happy when their families are excited and happy.

How can you create a partnership with families?

- Introduce yourself and tell about your own spiritual background. Name a person or persons in your past who had a great influence on your spiritual development.
- Share your goals and dreams for kids, kids ministry, and family involvement.
- Enlist the help of parents and families in planning, scheduling, and preparing for kids ministry. Ask them also for their continual prayers for your ministry.
- Regularly acknowledge your appreciation of families for their commitment to church and spiritual growth.
- Ask families for their input and feedback on kids events and activities.

- Respect families' personal needs and schedules. Don't overburden or undercut family time.
- Show genuine interest in families, and show respect and appreciation.

Equipping Parents to Be Spiritual Leaders

Families are the most influential teachers in children's lives. Experience and observation have shown that no other group of people or individual persons impact a child in the same way that a family does in the formational years from birth to adolescence.

Spiritual teaching and learning can and should begin in the early years of a child's life. Knowing the impact of families on children's emotional, physical, social, and mental development, we are challenged to help families know they are also the most important spiritual leaders and influencers for their children.

Spiritual teaching is intended to be woven into every facet of our lives—all day, every day, every night, anywhere. We are called to teach, guide, model, and lead so that generations to come will know the Lord and love Him. Recall in Deuteronomy 6:6–9 God's words to Moses and the Israelites: "These words that I am giving to you today are to be in your heart. Repeat them to your children. Talk about them when you sit . . . walk . . . lie down . . . get up. Bind them . . . write them. . . ."

How can you equip parents to become spiritual leaders in the home? Begin with parent education. You don't have to have a three-month-long intensive course, complete with homework and projects, to guide parents and equip them for Bible teaching and spiritual guidance. Try some of these simpler approaches to training, educating, and preparing parents:

- Send a parent e-mail encouraging parents to join you in a Deuteronomy partnership. Refer them to Deuteronomy 6:4–9.
- Distribute a list of easy-to-read books or articles that can help parents focus on being spiritual leaders in their homes.
- Plan a brief information session following a worship service. Provide a meal or snacks. (Don't forget arrangements for kids during this time.)
- Consider having a coffee and doughnut fellowship to share highlights of books, articles, or blogs.
- Plan a parent potluck event with a brief program on teaching spiritual truths to kids.
- Create a blog dedicated to sharing news and information with your kids' families. Occasionally include features that specifically address biblical and spiritual teaching at home.
- Inform parents of seminars, retreats, and conferences in your area that focus on families as spiritual leaders.
- Plan a parent "pair-and-share time," trading ideas for effective ways of Bible teaching.
- Ask parents to send you questions about spiritual growth and development. Address questions periodically through e-mails, blog posts, or posters in the hallways at church.
- Display parent helps and family guides related to the curriculum your kids ministry uses. For example, showcase parent magazines, take-home activity pages, family cards, and apps.

Finally, seek God's leadership in supporting and strengthening families in their efforts to lead and teach their children. Affirm families for commitment, consistency, and faithfulness to lead their children to God. And commit to pray for families!

What about Involving Parents?

by Rachel Coe

Building Relationships with Families

You just can't minister to kids without involving their families. Whether children in your ministry are "church kids" or "infrequent flyers" who drop in once in a while, someone has to decide to bring them to church. Every child—and every family represented—can be impacted and influenced.

> You just can't minister to kids without involving their families.

How can you make a difference in the lives of kids and their families and help them grow in faith? How can you create a desire for families to believe in kids ministry and the spiritual impact it has on their kids? Begin by building relationships.

Be genuine in your conversations with families.

Understand family dynamics and situations as much as possible.

Interact with family members both inside the church and outside in the community.

Love families!

Develop pathways for two-way communication.

Respect parents' choices and decisions regarding their children.

Engage families in kids ministry.

Laugh with kids and families and enjoy their real-life stories.

Always seek God's direction in approaching families regarding situations and concerns related to kids.

Trust God for wisdom in strengthening families through kids ministry.

Involve seasoned and respected older adults as mentors and guides to parents and families.

Offer opportunities for families to connect with other families.

Notice families and help them feel important and appreciated.

Share good news with families and celebrate key events in their lives.

Help families discover ways to walk through crises and stressful situations.

Instill a spirit of fellowship among families.

Pray for families, kids, and their needs.

Share the love of Jesus with families through your kids ministry.

Conversations in the Hallway

And the grocery store . . . and the ballpark . . . and the playground.

Many times I've been walking down the hallway at church when a parent has stopped me to ask a question or make an observation. Almost always, that question had something to do with their child.

As a kids ministry leader, you will be approached often with questions. Some of the questions will be easy to answer; others will be "I'll get back with you on that" types of queries. Regardless of the question, it is clear the parent has confidence in you and trusts you.

Parents will learn whether you care about their child and their family. What steps can you take to build confidence in parents and instill in them a sense of trust in you?

- Be open to conversations with families. Don't just nod your head and walk on. Stop to chat with a family whether you are in the church hallway or grocery store aisle.
- Send cards to families to celebrate important life events or occasions. Always remember to acknowledge children's birthdays.
- Send a brief e-mail to families to tell them about upcoming events related to kids ministry.
- Occasionally showcase kids and families in a short video to play during church fellowship meals or at the welcome station in the kids area.
- Call a family to give support during times of crisis or need.

Simple conversations, casual encounters, and genuine interest in families will bring blessings to families and kids ministers!

What about Expectant Parents?

by Delanee Williams

Becoming new parents can be overwhelming. A church has an opportunity to minister, serve, and come alongside these parents. Leaders can gain parents' trust by building relationships with them even before their baby is born or adopted. Creating ministries for new and expectant parents is a way to build relationship with parents.

A new and expectant parent ministry is a connection point. It's an opportunity for churches to impact new parents in the church and in the community. Follow the steps listed below to begin this impactful ministry in your church.

- **Communicate the need for the ministry to the pastor and other church leadership.** Pray and share the vision of why this ministry is important. Communicate stories of families who are expecting in your church. Give the ministry a name such as First Contact or Cradle Connection.

- **Enlist a coordinator and ministry team.** The coordinator leads the ministry team working hand-in-hand with the preschool/children's minister. She performs the day-to-day details of the ministry such as making the initial contact with expectant parents and planning events. The coordinator enlists encouragers to serve on the ministry team. These encouragers are assigned to an expecting couple.

- **Discover names of prospective couples.** Create avenues for members to share names of expectant parents in the church (including themselves) and families in the community who may not be connected to a church.

- **Initiate contact by coordinator.** The coordinator makes an introductory call to gather information such as due date and learn of ways to pray for the expectant parents. Then, the coordinator assigns an encourager to each set of expectant parents.

- **Encourager contacts parents during the pregnancy or adoption process.** During the months leading up to the baby's arrival, the encourager builds a relationship with the couple through visits, calls, writing cards, and praying for them.

- **Visit the family when the baby arrives.** Schedule a time to visit the family. Depending on their schedule and situation, you may visit the hospital or at their home. Take small gifts for the parents such as a copy of *BabyLife* or *ParentLife* magazines. Possible gifts for the baby include baby care items, a blanket, or small remembrance. Don't forget to include the siblings. Bubbles, a book, or other age-appropriate toys show that you care about the brothers and sisters too.

- **Celebrate the baby's arrival.** Consider ordering reusable yard signs to place in the family's yard for a couple of weeks after the baby's birth. Make sure to get permission from the family before placing the sign in the yard.

- **Prepare for other aspects of the expectant parent ministry.** Be prepared to minister to families in all situations. Include an encourager on your ministry team to serve families who have babies with special needs. Also, add an encourager who can minister to families who experience a miscarriage or stillbirth.

- **Follow up with parents.** A few weeks after the birth of the baby, the assigned encourager visits the new parents. She uses this opportunity to check with the parents to learn of any new ways the church can minister to them, pray for them, and answer any questions they may have about the preschool ministry.

Other Steps to Remember

- **Prepare a calendar for the year.** During the year, plan events such as moms' brunch, parents' dinner, or an ice cream sundae party for expectant and new parents (mom and dad) to attend. At these events, include a time of fellowship, relevant information for parents, and information about the church and pre-school ministry. Ask teachers from the babies' classes to share their testimony with the families. Explain what the babies experience in their classes on Sunday morning and how they are taught biblical truths in age-appropriate ways.

- **Prepare a budget.** When preparing a budget, remember to include small gifts for parents, babies, and siblings. In addition, estimate the costs of events and socials.

These steps can help to build a foundational relationship with the parents before the baby is born or arrives. Through an expectant parent ministry, your church can build trust, reach new families in the community, and build relationships with parents.

What about Equipping Families?

by Kayla Stevens

The heartbeat of kids ministry is to partner with families, but the pulse to live out this partnership can quickly fade. In our busy world, time is idolized, disinterest and complacency spread, and outsourcing a child's faith to the church abounds. It is tempting to allow discouragement to creep in and loosen our grip on this partnership.

Hold on tightly. In order to build a family ministry that outlasts us, we need to create a culture that elevates parents as spiritual leaders. Our job is to balance between leading kids and catalyzing opportunities to develop leaders of moms and dads. As you equip families, identify the consistent rhythms of your ministry that can help elevate parents as primary spiritual leaders.

Love Kids Loudly

Tangibly love kids in a way that is non-ignorable to families. Make the classroom experience memorable and valuable so kids leave excited and wanting more. Celebrate wins. Take five minutes to comment with fun social media posts. Show up to an occasional basketball game or dance recital. When you love kids loudly, you win parents' hearts. When you win their hearts, they will more seriously consider your words as you seek to equip.

Practice Availability

Availability communicates approachability. Building deep, trusting relationships with your families only happens through intentional availability. Invite different parents to lunch with you once a month. Connect with new families over frozen yogurt or game nights. Bring a parent along on your shopping trips for supplies. Listen to their stories and share what God is teaching you. As parents learn to trust you in the simple things, they will hear you clearer as you encourage their leadership in the hard things.

Create Heroes

Foster an atmosphere in your ministry of advocating for parents and grandparents. Create heroes, not to-do lists. Utilize small moments at pick up and drop off to brag on their kids or to engage them in authentic conversation. Resource parents with trustworthy tools that are applicable to their season and manageable to their schedules. Consider resources such as magazines (*ParentLife*), podcasts/blogs (*KidsMinistry 101*), or books (*Nothing Less*). Engage your parents and grandparents with achievable goals to fit their daily rhythms and applaud their wins.

Talk about What Matters

Recognize your limits in delicate conversations with kids. As you equip families, create opportunities to go deeper into sensitive topics with moms and dads. Don't shy away from hard conversations. This is where parents need biblical tools the most! Host a quarterly "Tough Talks" session. Invite preteen parents to a short-term study such as *Christ-Centered Parenting*. Create five-minute training videos to release to social media or repost helpful articles. As you partner with parents, recognize the teachable moments and lead them in biblical solutions to practice healthy conversations with their children.

Create More Ripples than Waves

Family discipleship occurs in small, sustainable repetitions. Cultivate expectations of parents that advance the ripples rather than the waves of your ministry. Sprinkle fun, excitement, and encouragement throughout the year through training meetings or conferences. As you do, make sure your waves fuel the small consistent ripples of family discipleship. Use kid-friendly devotional magazines such as *Bible Express* or *Adventure*. Point families to devotional apps like DevoHub. Explore *Foundations for Kids* or other Bible reading plans together. Advocate more for steadfast and repetitive discipleship opportunities that are reproducible at home.

Train with Innovation: Provide training opportunities that are innovative and practical. Lead monthly sessions for parents and grandparents through video chat meetings or conference calls. Utilize valuable tools such as Ministry Grid to train families from the comfort of their homes. Train as you go. Organize service opportunities, family mission trips, or nature hikes. Provide talking points for parents to practice engaging with their kids in spiritual conversations. Work to make your training opportunities both flexible and intentional for meeting families in their everyday lives.

If we desire to lead effectively, we must leverage our ministries for the kingdom, partnering with families and equipping them for this task. As you equip, take steps to cultivate a culture of discipleship, partnership, and leadership. You are in this together. Seek out the support of your pastor and other church leadership. Pray and plan for opportunities to equip families and implement strategies. Prioritize loving care for the whole family. When you do, you will elevate the partnership with your parents within your ministry, equipping them for transformational leadership that lasts.

CHAPTER 8

WHAT ABOUT THE HARD STUFF?

MINISTERING IN DIFFICULT SITUATIONS

Introduction

The pastor called and said, "I need you to meet me at the Browns' home. There's been a horrible accident and the family needs us now."

Arriving at that home and walking through their door, I found a husband and two preschool children huddled together, confused and in shock at the reality that their mom had tragically passed away and would not be coming home. That day was one of the hardest days I've ever experienced in ministry.

It was several months later (and still now, many years later) that I realized just what a privilege it was to be with that young family. When folks open themselves up and allow you to walk alongside them during the hard times, they give you the most personal gift that could ever be given. Sharing in crisis, hospitalization, the death of a loved one, and even helping someone move to the end of their own life, is a gift that few receive.

This chapter is dedicated to helping equip you to be ready for the hard stuff. I pray you'll see these difficult situations as holy opportunities that allow you to live out the love, grace, and mercy that we've been extended. I pray that you will become Christ's love to those who need you most.

What about Ministry?

by Jeremy Carroll

Am I a minister? Am I a director? Is there a difference? If so, how does this difference translate into purpose and day-to-day responsibilities? If you have either of these words in your title, you have probably asked, or at least thought about, these questions.

The simple answer for most kids ministry leaders is you are both a minister and director. They can be seen as two sides of the same coin in kids ministry leadership.

Broadly speaking, these terms have connotations for day-to-day tasks. For the purposes of this book, we will talk about them in this way: The term "director" refers to the administrative side of planning and overseeing events and programs; the term "minister" refers to the spiritual responsibilities of disciple-making, service, and spiritual investment in children, their parents, and volunteers.

From a church organizational standpoint, churches often have blurry lines between the terms "minister" and "director" in position titles, making it difficult to understand your position within the staff, those you serve, and peers from other churches. In some cases, churches will differentiate between titles based on ordination and education. It is not the purpose of this book to discuss whether there is merit to that differentiation. It will be most helpful to you to determine what your supervisor's expectations are.

While we cannot address the specifics of how your church approaches your specific job description, we want to help you sort through how your regular tasks relate to being a minister or a director.

In a basic sense, as a part of God's church, you are definitely a minister. This calling expands beyond the scope of paid versus unpaid leadership positions. All believers can be understood as ministers in the broad definition of "one who serves." As Christians, we are all servants of Jesus and should serve others. Ephesians 4 describes how all members of the body are gifted for the work of ministry. Some who are gifted have the gifts of equipping others for the work of the ministry. These groups of people are often called "ministers." And all of us, Paul says in 2 Corinthians 5, are "ministers of reconciliation."

As mentioned above, "director" can be specifically related to the administrative side of your ministry. These responsibilities, such as budgeting, purchasing curriculum, enlisting volunteers, and planning special events are necessary parts of your ministry. If you have an active ministry, these types of tasks must be done. Often it falls to the children's director to take care of these details personally.

Regardless of your official title, you are likely in your role because you believe you are called to be there. And according to your specific giftedness, you may enjoy one side of your job more than the other. However, both are important parts of serving in a church and leading a ministry. Once you have a clear understanding from your supervisor of his expectations, you will likely feel more prepared to accomplish the ministerial and directorial responsibilities. At the end of the day, you must strive to meet the expectations of your supervisor while balancing God's call to love people and serve them.

What about Crises?

by Bill Emeott

When working to help children in your ministry deal with a crisis situation, always take into consideration the general characteristics of the child (or children) to whom you are ministering. Consider the mental and emotional maturity of that child. Be sensitive to a child's right to fear, grieve, and hurt. Understand that processing a crisis will be unique for each child, and it may not look like you think it should.

Generally speaking, most preschoolers and young kids may not even be aware of a public crisis. In some of those situations, ignorance may be the best plan. However, in today's media-driven world, there's a good chance they'll hear and—at some

> Processing a crisis will be unique for each child.

level—begin to be curious. (Be careful about the amount of media exposure and the adult conversations to which kids are exposed.) For those of us who have the privilege of walking alongside children during times of crisis, we should be ready to have meaningful conversations.

Below are some ideas that might help ministry leaders as they help families deal with children during times of crisis.

Be Sensitive: I believe that God gives us, by His Holy Spirit, a sense, a tug that leads us when we're careful to listen. Be especially sensitive to His guidance during tragedy and crisis. Beg Him to lead you as you offer advice and comfort. God wants you to be successful in leading children through crises. He wants you to "say the right thing." Start with prayer.

Be Talkative: Talk with children. Include them (when appropriate) in discussions regarding the crisis. Find appropriate opportunities to talk about the situation and encourage parents to do the same (around the dinner table, when tucking your child in for bed, in the car while driving to school). Most children are talkative by nature. Take advantage of this time to share and talk.

Be Quiet: I know I just told you to be talkative, but part of the balance of walking with a child through a crisis is learning when to talk and when to just be quiet. There are no easy answers here, and it's not always black-and-white. You'll learn more and more through experiences when to speak and when to just sit and be quiet. Don't try to fix the situation too quickly with words. Your presence may be all that's needed for the moment.

Be Honest: Tell the truth. Don't deny that something bad has happened. Be honest with yourself. Recognize your own feelings. Understand that you have feelings regarding the crisis too. Know how you feel and understand that your feelings play a part in shaping a child's feelings.

Be Respectful: Ask children how they feel about the crisis and be respectful of their feelings. Realize that everyone's feelings are real, so validate their emotions. Kids may not process a crisis in the same way that adults do, but that's okay! Give children permission to feel the feelings that they have.

Be Age-Appropriate: Each child develops at different rates. Be intentional about knowing the development of the child you're counseling and their level of understanding. Some guidelines to follow might include the avoidance of euphemisms and complicated explanations. Answer the questions asked while being careful not to overload a child with too much information. If they want to know and you've created an atmosphere of freedom to ask, they will!

Be Reassuring: Reassure children that it's going to be okay. Assure them that they are safe. Many children may begin to fear leaving the presence of significant adults in their lives. Honestly assure them that their feelings are important and that you (and those to whom you entrust them) are concerned with their safety. If you're visually frightened, a child is likely to assume your fears.

> God is in control. He will use this crisis for His good.

Be Hopeful: Support a child as she works through the emotions of a crisis. Expect her to be concerned but offer her the hope that we have as Christians. Explain that God is in control. He will use this crisis for His good. We may not understand His ways, but we can trust His heart. Pray with children.

Teach children to seek God for their strength, especially in crises. Allow this time to grow them as followers of Jesus.

Allow times of crisis to bring you closer to Him as your Deliverer and Savior. Allow God to use times of crisis to bring you closer as a family. Use these teachable moments to demonstrate that the God we serve and the faith we teach are real.

What about Hospitals?

by Delanee Williams

As a staff member, hospital visitation may be one of your responsibilities. You may enjoy this aspect of your job, but most feel uncomfortable and experience anxiousness. The patient may be someone you know well or someone you've never met. The visit may be a celebratory time, such as a birth of a child, or it may be a stressful time, such as a surgery or terminal illness.

Consider these tips as you visit people in the hospital:

- If you're sick or not feeling well, wait until you are well to visit the patient.
- Before visiting, know as much about the patient as possible.
- Learn about the nature of the patient's illness.
- Check at the nurses' station to see if it's an appropriate time for your visit. Meal times are generally not good visitation times.
- Upon entering the room, be in line with the patient's vision.

- Stand in a place you are able to quickly step out if necessary. If medical personnel enter the room during the visit, politely offer to step outside.

- Notice what the patient and the patient's room look like; these details can communicate how the patient is feeling. Be observant of medical equipment in the room.

- Introduce yourself—who you are, where you are from, why you are there, and so on.

- If the patient has family members or friends present, include them in your introduction.

- Be a good listener. Hear what the patient and family members are saying and communicating to you.

- Try not to whisper or talk softly to another person in the patient's room. This can cause the patient anxiety.

- Be yourself, and be genuine.

- Before holding a baby, wash your hands with soap and water in the sight of the parents.

- In most situations, patients in the hospital need rest; therefore, keep visits brief.

- Pray with the patient during your visit. Ask, "How can I pray for you?"

- If the patient is sleeping or unable to have visitors, leave a short note or card with your contact information.

- Keep information confidential.

By making hospital visits, you're able to minister to individuals and families. Be sensitive to the Holy Spirit moving and know the Lord is using you as you care and connect with people.

What about Death?

by William Summey

Five Things Adults Must Know

1. Children experience loss in many ways, not just through death. Any significant change in their circumstances (for example: moving, a significant illness, family financial difficulties, etc.) can result in feelings of loss as significant for a child as that of a death.

2. Adults need to be aware that grief is a normal emotional response to death, even for children. Children can experience the range and intensity of emotions that adults feel following a death.

3. Children are never too young to grieve. Children will have questions and need guidance, comfort, and direction to move forward.

4. The reactions of a child to a death in the family are influenced most by the surviving family members and how the family is restructured after that death. Some factors that determine a child's reaction to a death are the relationship of the child to the deceased, the reaction of the family, the resources the family has, and the family support system, particularly the church.

5. Recognize common myths that derail our efforts to effectively deal with grief.

Myth: Adults can easily explain death to children.
Truth: There is no standard way to explain death.

Myth: The experience of grief has orderly stages.
Truth: Grief is unique to each person.

Myth: The grief of adults does not affect the bereaved child.

Truth: Children are attentive to adults' speech, feelings, and actions.

Myth: Adults should avoid topics that cause a child to cry.
Truth: Children need to grieve as adults do.

Myth: An active, playing child is not a grieving child.
Truth:: Many children actually act out their grief while playing.

Myth: Children need to get over their grief and move on.
Truth:: No one gets over grief. They learn to live with grief in healthy ways. Ignoring grief is never healthy.

Myth: Children are better off not attending funerals.
Truth: Children need to learn the reality of death as part of life. They can be prepared for this stressful and painful experience by explaining beforehand what they will see, how the body will look and feel, who will be there, and what will take place. However, be prepared to leave with the child if needed.

Three Things Adults Must Do

1. Talk to your child. The way adults tell a child about a death is important.

- Talk to the child as soon as possible.
- Give the child a simple, honest explanation using clear, concise words.
- Find familiar surroundings to talk.
- Use age-appropriate words.

- Give adequate but not detailed information about the death.
- Address the child's fears and anxieties.
- Reassure the child that he is not to blame for the death and that someone will care for him.
- Listen carefully to the child, validating feelings, assisting with overwhelming emotions, and involving him in the process.
- Continue, as closely as possible, the child's routine.
- Model appropriate grief behaviors.
- Provide opportunities to remember the loved one who has died.

2. Children experience grief differently according to many factors. The following are general descriptions of how children experience grief by age:

- Infants and toddlers express their pain with sadness, crying, difficulty sleeping or eating, or clinging behavior.
- Children two to seven years of age may believe they caused the death. Other emotional responses include regression, lack of feeling, explosive emotions, fear, acting out, guilt, and sadness. Children at this age need constant reassurance and repeated explanations.
- By seven to eight years of age, children know that death is irreversible, inevitable, and universal.

3. Children have to understand, grieve, remember, and find a way to go on with life. Sensitive adults can assist children by modeling healthy ways to express grief, providing a safe place to process feelings, being willing to listen well to children's stories of loss, and utilizing methods to help children express their thoughts and feelings. We help

as we listen, tell stories, create art, play, view pictures, write music, and utilize other creative ways for children to express and process their feelings. Grieving the death of a pet, friend, family member, grandparent, or parent is a continual task throughout life because loss and grief due to death are a normal part of living. Know when to refer the child to counseling. Ask questions. Bereavement in early childhood can have a damaging effect. Children who experience loss need to express their grief and work through unresolved feelings in order to prevent the possibility of later problems. They might benefit from referral to a skilled counselor, peer groups, or family therapy.

What about Special Situations?

---

by Jeff Land

In your ministry to children, you will be faced with many different scenarios. While some situations will be once-in-a-lifetime, there are some situations that you can expect to happen repeatedly in your ministry. Some reoccurring situations that you will likely be faced with are ministering to adoptive families, ministering to military families, and ministering to families affected by divorce.

Ministering to Adoptive and Fostering Families

Be aware of attachment.

Kids who are adopted have spent an amount of time in their lives away from the people they now call family. Due to this time spent away, there may be attachment difficulties on both sides. An adoptive child may struggle to attach to his father because he's been surrounded by caregivers who are women for his entire life. An adoptive mother may struggle with feelings of guilt for not feeling more attached to her child.

Providing a safe place for the child is important. Think about your volunteer leadership and consider if you will be able to provide a consistent leader in that newly adopted child's life so that positive relationships can be built. Support the parents who are struggling to connect with their newly adopted child with materials and resources.

> Providing a safe place for the child is important.

Understand each child's background.

Children who are adopted often bring with them hurts, emotions, and other insecurities. Learning about the child's background will help you know how to appropriately correct behavior in situations where it is necessary. An adopted child in your church is living a different life from the one that she had lived previously. She may now have access to food, clothing, and other materials in a way that she has never had before.

Be sensitive.

Being sensitive to the child might sound obvious, but it's worth mentioning. Be sensitive in the way you talk to the child. Never address a parent or child—either birth, adoptive, or fostering—as "real," i.e., "Which of your kids are *really* yours?" Be sensitive to a child's past. Children adopted from other countries may not yet understand customs and traditions of the church. Be sensitive to a child's need for privacy. Adoption stories seem to be widely shared in society today, but remember: it's not your place to ask a child to share about his adoption. If he wants to share, let him, but if he just wants to be a fourth grader with his buddies, that's fine too!

Celebrate.

Remember that families who adopt should be celebrated in the same way that a newborn is celebrated. Newly adoptive parents face many struggles that parents of newborns face. Bringing meals, welcome home gifts, and sending information about child dedication are all ways that you can minister to the adoptive parents. Remember that even if a child is a little older when she is adopted, the new parents will be excited to see that you recognize their family has grown.

Ministering to Military Families

Build inclusive relationships.

Military families are used to moving around. They have committed to serving their country and they should be honored for their service. They are real people and they desire to build friendships with their new friends. Sometimes it is easy for groups within the church to feel unwelcoming to newcomers. For military families, they do not have the luxury of time to really develop a new group within the church. Help connect military parents in established groups that are inclusive of newcomers. Likewise, help military children assimilate into your group as quickly as possible.

Support the family at home.

While military families are each unique, a commonality they share is the fact that at some point, one or both parents might be deployed. This time can be especially tough for the parent and children who are left at home. Provide support by thinking of special ways to remember the parent and the children. Check in and find out if there are ways that your church can be ministering more effectively to the family during this time.

Remember them when they are gone.

One of the joys of ministry is the development of lifelong relationships with brothers and sisters in Christ. Many times, children in military families can struggle with leaving the strong friendships they have built during their two- to three-year assignment in your area. Do things to remember the children of military families after they have moved on to a new assignment. Send birthday cards, remember holidays, and send occasional postcards. You will never know the impact simple remembrances will make on the child and her parents.

Ministering to Families Affected by Divorce

Remember holidays can hurt.

No child asks to come from a family where divorce has occurred. For many, the holidays can be an especially painful time of remembering the way things used to be. Children may want to avoid talking about or participating in holiday-related activities. Encourage children to explore their feelings and allow them to talk with you about their hurts. Sometimes, after divorce, one parent might distance himself from the child. Remember this as you plan events, and be sensitive to kids who might need to borrow a dad for a special event.

Encourage children to explore their feelings.

Be consistent.

Children may be embarrassed about their parents' divorce. They may feel like it's their fault. Be a consistent force for those kids, letting them know that they are loved and accepted by you and your church. Newly single moms and dads have many responsibilities that they previously shared. A child may feel left out during this time. Your consistent love and care will help a child through this time.

Provide resources.

Be prepared as a resource for parents and children who are facing divorce. Being knowledgeable about issues surrounding divorce and grief support can be very helpful. Have a list of Christian counselors who focus on helping children. If the need is there, you might consider offering a divorce support group for children. There are many resources available. Choose resources that are reputable and come from a source that you trust.

What about Referring?

by Melita Thomas

Child abuse is a scary topic. It's certainly something you hope to never deal with in your church. But the likelihood of crossing paths at some point in your ministry with children who are experiencing some form of abuse is unfortunately high. These kids will need someone vigilant enough to recognize the signs of abuse who will do what it takes to shelter them when no one else can or will.

As a kids ministry leader, it is your responsibility to protect and advocate for the children in your care. It is *not* your responsibility to determine whether or not abuse actually occurred or to find proof of abuse. That is for professionals to determine. But it *is* your responsibility, under child welfare laws, to report *reasonable suspicions* of abuse and neglect to local child protective services agencies.

Here are the first steps to take:

- **Get to know the laws in your state.** Every state is different, but many states classify anyone who works with children, including church volunteers and staff, as a mandatory reporter. That means they are legally required to report any suspected child abuse to law enforcement or family services—even (and perhaps especially) if a pastor or ministry leader tells them not to.

- **Check with your church's legal counsel and/or insurance carrier.** They can advise you regarding responsibility for reporting suspected abuse.
- **Educate yourself and your volunteers.** Enroll in abuse awareness and prevention training. Many reputable agencies exist to help church leaders learn what to look for and how to respond when a child is being hurt.
- **Use best practices** (such as enforcing "the two-person rule" so that a minor is never left alone with only one adult) to protect children against abuse and volunteers from any accusation of abuse.
- **Run background checks** on *every* volunteer and paid worker involved in ministry with minors.
- **Include a plan for reporting abuse** as part of your ministry's policies and procedures.

What Constitutes Child Abuse and Neglect?

There are four major types of abuse commonly recognized. Often, two or more occur together.

1. **Neglect** is the most common form of child mistreatment. It involves the failure to provide adequate food, clothing, shelter, supervision, education, guidance, emotional support, or medical care.
2. **Physical abuse** includes non-accidental inflicted injuries, ranging from bruises to burns, broken bones,

abusive head trauma (also known as Shaken Baby Syndrome), and death. Causing bodily injury to a child is considered abuse, even if the caregiver did not intend to cause harm when using corporal punishment.

3. **Sexual abuse** refers to any type of sexual act that involves a child—including indecent exposure, physical sexual contact, or using a child to produce child pornography. In most instances, the offender is someone the child knows and trusts.

4. **Emotional abuse** (or psychological abuse) includes excessive yelling and intimidation; criticizing and belittling; and withholding of warmth, love, attention, praise, and encouragement. Emotional abuse almost always accompanies other forms of abuse and can be difficult to prove.

When Should I Report Abuse?

Report abuse when you . . .

- Witness someone hitting a child (including with an object).
- See bruises or other marks that do not appear to be the result of an accident.
- Are told by a child that he or she has been harmed by someone.
- Are aware that a young child has been left unsupervised or appears undernourished.

What Do I Do if I Suspect Abuse or Neglect?

- Document (in writing) the facts and observations that led to your suspicions.
- Call your state or local Department of Children's Services report hotline (available online) to report abuse or suspicions of abuse.
- Contact the Childhelp National Child Abuse Hotline at 1-800-4-A-CHILD (1-800-422-4453). This hotline is staffed twenty-four hours a day, seven days a week, with professional crisis counselors who have access to a database of 55,000 emergency, social service, and support resources. All calls are anonymous.

You do not have to give your name when reporting suspected child abuse or neglect, and cannot be held liable for damages under criminal or civil law. A social worker will listen to your concerns and decide if a formal report and investigation are warranted.

Other Things to Keep in Mind

- Keep your immediate supervisor in the loop. Understanding, grace, forgiveness, and love will be critical to the process of healing and restoration for a victim of abuse and his or her family, but you should also remember that extending grace, forgiveness, and love does not always mean the situation returns to what it was before or during the abuse. God is a God of justice and grace, and we ought to reflect both of those characters, seeking justice for the abused and extending appropriate gestures of grace to abusers.
- If the suspected abuse involves a volunteer or staff member, immediately remove the individual from

working with children pending the resolution of an investigation.

- Notify parents as appropriate. (Exercise caution when the suspected abuse or neglect was, or may have been, at the hands of parents.)

CHAPTER 9

HOW CAN WE ALL GET ALONG?

NAVIGATING RELATIONSHIPS IN MINISTRY

Introduction

"I'd love ministry if it weren't for the people!"

It had been an especially difficult Sunday and our student pastor and I were having hot fudge ice cream cakes in an attempt to heal from the beating we'd taken. That day a group of volunteers came with a list of things they thought we could do better. They were sure we needed their advice and counsel but (guess what) they didn't offer their assistance. I laughed with him, but to be honest, there were times when I felt the exact same way.

We get the privilege of ministering to and with people: big people (parents, leaders, staff, fellow ministers) and little people (kids). Each of those people is unique, and unique people have unique perspectives, unique preferences, and unique and sometimes differing opinions. That's good! God has done a masterful job of putting the body together. Our responsibilities include working toward understanding, appreciating, and getting along with unique people.

Ministry without people isn't ministry at all. It's just useless programming. Ministry needs people—all kinds of people. So, we do what we need to do to figure folks out and cultivate healthy relationships. We show them we care. We show them we appreciate them, and we strive to understand them so we'll be found saying, "I love ministry because of the people!"

What about Communicating Effectively?

by Landry Holmes

Have you ever had that sick feeling in the pit of your stomach immediately after hitting "send" on an "I-just-need-to-vent" e-mail? Do you wonder why the recipient of your snarky text message doesn't reply? Have you found yourself debating a controversial issue on a Facebook thread? What about that time you tried to confront someone face-to-face and you froze or took a passive-aggressive approach?

If you've never experienced one of the situations above or something similar, then you may want to skip this section of the chapter. For the rest of us (and I am guessing that means all of us!), read on.

Today we have access to the most efficient communication tools in history. However, our communication skills are probably the worst they've ever been. In some ways, digital technology has made us poor communicators. Even when we try to converse face-to-face, the bad habits we have picked up from trying to communicate in 280 characters or less can interfere with constructive dialogue. In his letter to the Christians in Rome, Paul writes, "If possible, as far as it depends on you, live at peace with everyone" (Rom. 12:18). Living peacefully in community is only possible with good communication.

> The bad habits we have picked up from trying to communicate in 280 characters or less can interfere with constructive dialogue.

As kids ministry leaders, our professional community is comprised of our pastor and staff, teams, parents, and kids.

1. One communication principle applies to all three groups: always let people know what you are doing and why you are doing it. People are more apt to

follow your leadership if they know where you are going and why you are headed in that direction.

2. A second principle is to listen more than tell. If we want people to listen to us and, more important, if we want to be obedient to Paul's command to "consider others as more important" (Phil. 2:3) than ourselves, we need to listen to them first.

3. A third principle of effective communication is to use a variety of methods.

As alluded to previously, we have a vast communication arsenal. We tend to gravitate to one or two favorite ways to communicate according to our preferences and personality types, but we may need to broaden our forms of interaction. Here are seven modes of communication and when to use them:

- Texts—Send a text when you need to provide brief information or when you need to ask a simple question. Avoid texting complaints.

- Facebook posts—Post on Facebook when a group of individuals need to know something, or when you need donated items for a one-time project. Do not use Facebook to express controversial opinions or to "preach" against your pet peeve.

- Twitter—If you want several people to know about something and you can say it clearly and faithfully in 280 characters or less, then consider sending a tweet. Again, Twitter is not a platform to be a bully or to rant about an issue.

- E-mails—Today's parents are busy, and so is everyone else. E-mails are meant to inform, and should be short. Use bulleted text when possible. E-mails are excellent ways to let parents know what their children learned at church, as well as information about special events.

- Phone calls or video chats—The previous communication methods tend to be one-sided. If you want to have a discussion or enlist volunteers, then a phone call or prearranged video chat may be the best option.
- Face-to-face—This is the introvert's least favorite communication choice; however, it is biblical. John knew that face-to-face interaction was more effective than writing a letter (or sending an e-mail): "Though I have many things to write to you, I don't want to use paper and ink. Instead, I hope to come to you and talk face to face so that our joy may be complete" (2 John 12). Tony Reinke says, "there is something of us in written words, but not everything in true fellowship can be typed out on phone screens and sent at the speed of light through fiber-optic cables."[14] Always speak to someone face-to-face when you deliver a difficult message or when you need to address an uncomfortable subject.

Regardless of how we choose to communicate, we should always do so peaceably. Unfortunately, as kids ministry leaders, we can come across as whiners, and that causes people to stop listening to us. Practice saying, "Yes, we can do that and here's how," more than, "No, that won't work." Let your pastor and staff talk through suggestions that may impact kids ministry instead of trying to shut them down. Be an advocate for children without coming across as a naysayer. Encourage parents rather than chastising them, and talk to kids in a way that reminds them that God values and loves them. In so doing we can "live in harmony with one another" (Rom. 12:16a), and we will glorify God in our interactions with one another.

What about Difficult People?

by Klista Storts

So, what about difficult people? Surely you won't have any of those in a Christian kids ministry! Right?

Unfortunately, you are going to have to deal with some difficult people. After all, Christians and non-Christians alike are, indeed, human. We sin; we make mistakes; we miscommunicate; and we hurt each other—sometimes even with the best intentions. How can you face these obstacles and maintain your sanity, your faith, and your ministry?

1. **Pray.** Your first response, no matter who or what the problem is, should be prayer. Ask God to intervene in the situation. Prepare your heart to accept the remedy, no matter what. Sometimes His answer will be to change the opposing person's heart, and sometimes His answer will be to change yours.

2. **Look.** Ask God to help you see the situation through the eyes of the other party and, more important, through His. Often, when you are able to see and better understand the opposition's point of view, the solution for the problem seems clear. This stands true for issues you have with kids *and* adults!

3. **Listen.** In addition to seeing the situation from another perspective, you may need to stop talking and just listen. Too often, a person can be so busy stating his opinion or crafting his reply that he doesn't take time to truly hear what's on the other person's heart.

4. **Ask forgiveness.** Sometimes, you're the problem! Sometimes, you're just wrong. Do not hesitate to ask

forgiveness when you discover that you're the one at fault. You'll not only help defuse the situation, but you'll set an example, making it easier for others when they have to ask.

5. **Seek advice.** A person who feels undervalued often feels a need to devalue others. If someone frequently questions your work, your methods, or opinions, it is possible they have a need to be respected for their knowledge. You can help fill the void they sense by asking for their advice. It is okay to admit that you don't know everything there is to know. In fact, this humbling attribute draws people toward you instead of driving them away.

6. **Acknowledge the parent's role.** Time and again kids ministers say, "I love kids ministry . . . if it weren't for the parents." Parents rightly desire what is best for their kids—and they are the most important adults in their children's lives. Oftentimes their opinions are going to be different than yours. Be sure to respect the wishes of the parents as it pertains to their kids. However, don't make the mistake of letting a parent (or a few parents) take over your ministry or pull you away from your vision.

7. **Acknowledge your pastor's role.** God has placed your pastor in this church for this time. Your pastor is charged with leading . . . maybe sometimes without consulting you. Respect the position even if, and especially when, you're struggling with the person. When you do feel the need to speak up, don't whine and don't argue; simply state what you see as a problem and offer your help toward a solution.

8. **Surround yourself with people unlike you.** *What?* You have been gifted with a unique skill set. So have others in your church. If you are a "people pleaser," you may need to have a leader close to you who can help with the hard decisions. If you tend to be a "policy person," you may need others on your team who can help smooth ruffled feathers. Whatever your personality and giftedness, look for others with complementary talents.

9. **Release control.** If you have a strong team member with a tendency to try and overpower you on ministry issues, discover a project near to that member's heart and put her in charge of it. Be sure to place and explain boundaries for reporting back to you, but release as much control as you can. Remember, though, that ultimately, you will be responsible for the success of the project in your ministry.

10. When all else fails, smile, love the difficult people, and refer back to point number one!

What about Building Strong Relationships with Other Staff Members?

---

by Tim Pollard

Serving on a church staff is exciting, but as you have already discovered, church staffs are made up of real people. We all have our quirks and preferences, and sometimes we have to navigate a landscape that presents us with personalities that might not mesh well with our own. Building strong relationships with those with whom you serve is possible, and I'll see if I can do something to help you make those strong relationships with the other pastors on your staff.

Preschool/Children's Minister

If you are responsible for both preschool and children's ministries, hopefully it won't be hard for you to get along with yourself. If you are responsible for one area or the other, making bonds with the person in the other chair should be easy since, hopefully, you share the same passions and desires for boys and girls.

- Consider weekly (or daily) chats with the person who shares that passion with you.
- Make time weekly, if possible, and at least monthly, to connect for lunch or a little bit of a break in your action to get better acquainted.
- Intentionally make time for planning that will mutually benefit both preschoolers and kids.

Student Minister

We've probably heard the jokes about the relationships between youth ministers and kids ministers, but those jokes don't need to characterize the relationship you have with the youth minister on staff.

- Take the opportunity during staff meetings to champion your ministry.
- Be intentional when you talk with the youth minister, and ask how you can specifically prepare kids best to make the transition into the student ministry.
- Form a group of "tweens" or "preteens" that relate to both kids and student ministries. Working together with this age group will help you connect with the

youth minister and help you encourage kids as they transition to the next group.

Education Minister/Next Generation Pastor

In some churches the education minister may be responsible for oversight of your area. If that is the case in the ministry you serve, make sure that your interactions with this staff member are always professional and respectful.

- Take the opportunity during staff meetings to champion your ministry.
- Consider the education pastor's take on the preschool/children's ministry and be willing to take constructive criticism.
- Be firm in knowing that kids ministry is where God has called you and discuss issues openly and honestly.

Music Minister

You may not deal directly with the music minister (unless you work together to plan music for kids), but you can always make some time to connect with the music minister.

- Take the opportunity during staff meetings to champion your ministry.
- Connect intentionally with your music minister to plan activities and teaching that involve music and kids.
- Support the music ministry of your church in any way you can.

Senior Pastor

Depending on your ministry environment, you may serve with a pastor who is highly engaged or you may not.

- Take the opportunity during staff meetings to champion your ministry.
- Boldly share the plans you have for your ministry so that your senior pastor sees the value in the ministry you are involved in.
- Share your overall plan for the kids ministry with your pastor, and ask how he would like to be involved.

Be the Champion!

You saw those words repeated above and, in their intent, you see that if you exude the passion for your ministry in front of the other ministers on your staff, it will be easy for them to see the importance of training kids in the knowledge of the Lord so they will grow into faithful and fruitful church members.

Don't Be a Silo!

On many church staffs you get "silos" in which each ministry is working alone toward their own goal and not everyone is working together to accomplish one united goal. In instances like that, how can you eaffect change to break down the walls between those ministries and make the vision of the staff cohesive and viable?

- Much of this can be accomplished during staff meetings. If your staff regularly plans together, then be an agent for creating a united platform for teaching that incorporates the whole family of believers no matter their age.

- If your church staff does not meet together regularly, or you are not a part of that meeting, make it a point to keep other members of the staff involved in what you are planning.

- Attend events that are outside the scope of your ministry definition. What I mean by that is if the student ministry is having an event, or the worship ministry is having an event that gives you the freedom to attend, make a point to attend those events so that other ministries can see that you are interested and want to be involved in their ministries. It might just give them the spur they need to make the same choices in some of your events.

Gender Dynamics

If you are a female working with an all-male staff, that can sometimes be a challenge. Since I have no authority on the subject, I've asked several of my female friends to give some advice in handling situations on staff that arise from these dynamics.

- Be yourself. Don't try and be "one of the boys" unless that's really your personality. Being real is the best way to fit in on the staff.

- Be careful. Don't get involved in lots of dynamics that put you into uncomfortable situations. Be sure you always put yourself in situations that pair you with more than one individual. If you are in one-on-one meetings, make sure your door is open and others can see any interactions that are happening.

- Texting is something else you may want to consider carefully. If you need to text someone on staff who is a male, ask his wife if she wants to be included in those texts. Do everything you can to be transparent and make wives feel comfortable with their husbands working with the only female on staff.

What about Friendships?

by Shelly Harris

Is it possible to be surrounded by kids, parents, and volunteers yet still feel unconnected to your church? Yes. Kids ministry is busy. By the time you take snacks to the three-year-olds, help a teacher with a discipline problem in third grade, and find a last-minute substitute for the second service crawlers room, you are tired. One way to stay refreshed is through friendships.

Building friendships at church can be hard, but a church is a community, and you are a part of that community. Here are some ideas to help you connect with people in your church community:

- **Pray for God to help you connect with people.** It's so simple, but sometimes we forget to stop and pray for what we need. Ask God to provide and to open your eyes and heart to see who He puts in your path.
- **Know your team.** Get to know the people who serve in the kids ministry. Host a fellowship, go out for coffee with someone, or eat a meal with a few families. Learn about who they are and why they are serving in kids ministry. Share your passion for kids ministry.

- **Get outside your ministry.** Attend some (not all!) events that aren't kids ministry specific. You need to meet people outside your ministry. Get to know the senior adults. They have loads of wisdom to glean from. Get to know college students. They have loads of passion to glean from. Get to know your fellow staff members. They have loads of insight about your church to glean from.

- **Open up.** Extroverts will have no problem with this. Introverts will have to make an effort to open up and let people get to know them. Part of community is sharing your life with people. If the only time people hear you speak is to ask for volunteers, they will soon tune you out. People need to know you, not just your ministry.

- **Be smart.** There are some things your fellow church members do not need to hear you vent about. Call a trusted mentor or fellow friend in ministry for those times. Being "real" does not mean sharing everything you experience, feel, or think.

> People need to know you, not just your ministry.

- **Boundaries are good.** Be wise about opposite-sex friendships. Set boundaries and keep them. The same is true for people who are negative or draining. Not everyone needs to be your best friend and vice versa.

- **Remember that friendships take time.** It's a process. Be intentional about the process, but don't feel pressured to rush it.

What about Church Influencers?

by Jeremy Carroll

Every church has key influencers who may not be paid staff members. It is typically easy to spot these men and women, yet it can be difficult to know how to build authentic relationships with them because they may not be directly involved in your ministry.

These influencers could include an older man in the congregation who has been a pillar in your community for many years. Or maybe a grandmotherly figure who has cared for many of the church leaders as they have grown up in the community. The person could be in an official position, like chairman of deacons, elder, or just someone who people look to for important decisions. Regardless of their role, building genuine relationships with key influencers will both help your ministry and enrich you personally.

Something to remember: If the person truly has influence within your church, they likely approved of your hiring or placement. This means he recognized value in placing you in that position and either initiated your placement or was part of the approval process. And if he sees value in you holding your position, he sees value in you as a person too.

How can you do this?

Be intentional. Take the initiative. Keep him in the loop and encourage him as a champion of your ministry. Take him for coffee once a month or every couple of months, and share your heart and the exciting things that are coming up in your ministry. Share your wins and what God is doing in the lives of the children in your ministry. Help him see the real lives being touched by the gospel. The more you share, the more your ministry will be on his heart and he will appreciate the value of what you do. If you have a large group time in your kids ministry and he is comfortable talking to a group, invite him to guest teach a class or just sit in and observe sometime.

Be humble. When you meet with him, ask questions too. Sincerely inquire what God is doing in other ministries of the church. Listen to him. Learn from him. Yes, you are the champion for your ministry, but there will be much wisdom you can glean from his experiences. Be humble.

Finally, **be gracious.** When he speaks up on your behalf, send him a thank-you card and say thank you when you pass him in the hallway.

Your ministry is ultimately in the hands of God. He has placed you in a local body of believers that is designed to encourage and support you. As you build authentic relationships with church influencers in your local congregation, expect God to teach you, challenge you, and, hopefully, encourage you as well.

CHAPTER 10

WHAT ABOUT ME?

BALANCING LIFE IN MINISTRY

Introduction

January is officially VBS season for me. I know that sounds weird, but it's in January that I am involved in eight national VBS training events and, as you might guess, most of November and December are focused on getting ready for January. It's a hard (but fun) season that takes most of my attention.

There are very busy seasons in the life of a kids ministry leader. There are times when you're pushed hard and the hours needed won't match the hours available. There will be times when your ministry will call you away from your family or other important parts of your life. Learn to balance. Learn to look forward and prepare or pay it back afterwards. Balance is key. In Ecclesiastes 3:1 we read that "there is an occasion for everything, and a time for every activity under heaven."

The reality is that other "focuses" in my life don't go away during VBS season. I have to keep those plates spinning too. Balancing on-going programing, ministry needs, and special events with family, personal worship, and fun are important and crucial to ministry success.

What about My Calling?

by Debbie Ruth

Do you remember the story from Exodus of how God called Moses to lead the Israelites? After God called to Moses from the burning bush, God explained that He wanted Moses to lead the Israelites. Moses responded by saying, "Who am I that I should go?" (Exod. 3:11).

This may be your thought today about your role in kids ministry. You may be asking yourself, "Who am I to lead this ministry?" or "Why would You ask *me* to do this?" Truly, the call of God to any task is important, and a call to kids ministry is especially important. After all, He has called you to a ministry that will shape the lives of some of His most precious creations: children and their families!

There are a few things we can remember from the story of Moses:

God spoke to Moses, and Moses listened. God spoke to Moses and addressed his fears. Though Moses continued to have doubts and mention them to God, God continually reminded Moses that God is the One doing the work. God told Moses, "This is what you are to say to the Israelites: I AM has sent me to you" (Exod. 3:14). God calls and equips, and He does this even through our doubts and fears.

So, whom are you listening to? God has spoken to us in His Word, and He still speaks through what He has spoken. If God has called you to this work, He will be faithful to guide you in every step. Lean into Him by continually going back to His Word and prayer; learn to trust His voice.

God equipped Moses with the tools he needed for the job. When Moses asked, "What if they won't believe me?" (Exod. 4:1), God showed Moses the tools already provided for him.

If God has called you to this work, He is equipping you with tools to do the tasks. Think about your gifts and abilities. Are you using them wisely as you work with kids, parents, and leaders?

God called Moses to step beyond what he considered comfortable and easy to do. Over and over, Moses took risks, but the risks he took were not foolish or without caution, because God was at work through him.

> If God has called you to this work, He is equipping you with tools to do the tasks.

If God has called you to this work, take wise steps of faith after much prayer and planning. Don't take on risks by yourself. Bring your leaders into the decision-making process. They can surround you with different perspectives and prayer. Reach out to kids ministers in other churches for support and attend conferences that will encourage you and strengthen your call.

God promised Moses that He would be with Moses. After God told Moses what He wanted him to do, God said, "I will certainly be with you" (Exod. 3:12). The task of leading the Israelites out of slavery surely must have been hard for Moses to grasp, yet God was with Moses every day, through every obstacle Pharaoh tried to throw his way.

If God has called you to this work, He has not left you. God knows the obstacles and the difficulty of the work. Revisit the time that God first called you to kids ministry and remember His clear direction. Then resist the lies of the enemy that would have you doubt this call. Seek Him in the daily stuff and long-term decisions, and trust His hand. "He who calls you is faithful; he will do it" (1 Thess. 5:24).

What about My Spiritual Growth?

by Bekah Stoneking

Most of my classes in seminary began the same way: the professor reviewed the syllabus, and then warned us to not allow our schoolwork to replace our personal time with the Lord.

Work that is spiritual in nature—whether it is schoolwork or ministry prep—is good work, but it is just that—work! It is not devotional time spent communing with the Lord and being changed by His Word.

I was able to heed my professors' warnings. However, I have other challenges regarding my spiritual growth. My proclivity is to allow my calendar to rule my quiet time. Busyness and tiredness tempt me to view my spiritual growth as just another to-do list item. To combat this, I've had to learn to say "no" to good things so I can say "yes" to great things and "yes" to the best thing—being still and knowing the Lord.

So what about you? Are you tempted to use your prep time as quiet time? Do you—actively or passively—live as if you do not need to regularly dwell in the Word? Are you like me with a weedy calendar that tries to choke out your devotions?

Whatever your temptations or proclivities, consider the ways you may build healthy spiritual rhythms.

Cultivate Spiritual Disciplines

Throughout the Bible, we see God communicating with His people. Communication is a key part of following and obeying God. We do this through prayer and Bible reading.

Prayer

What a gift it is that we have access to the Father by the finished work of the Son! And what a gift it is that the Spirit groans on our behalf when we find ourselves without the words to pray. If God communes with Himself, how much more should we—as finite, created ones—run to His feet in prayer? So run! Bathe your ministry and every step you take in prayer.

These ideas have helped me as I think about prayer:

- John Piper describes prayer as a walkie-talkie connecting the people on the ground with their commander during war.[15]
- Tim Keller is quoted saying that the only one audacious enough to wake a king at 3:00 a.m. for a glass of water is His child.
- Mark DeVries says that prayer is like breathing for your soul.[16]

Whether you're in the trenches of ministry or basking on a mountaintop, connect with God. Let your soul breathe. Talk with Him anytime about what is on your mind (nothing is too great or too small; remember that glass of water!).

> Prayer reminds us of our dependence upon God, and it is one of the most powerful tools we have.

Prayer reminds us of our dependence upon God, and it is one of the most powerful tools we have. It is not weak or passive to pray; it should be our first response in every situation! To help capture and focus my attention from the very start of the day, I write my prayer points on my bathroom mirror. That way, I can see them as I am getting ready. You might decide to write yourself a note and leave it in your pocket or tape it to the wall. Give yourself tangible reminders as you cultivate your prayer habits and practice praying without ceasing.

Bible Reading

God has given us His full counsel and the perfect revelation of Himself in Scripture. Knowing God's Word and being transformed by it is vital to our personal discipleship and in our disciple-making. Develop the discipline of regularly being in the Word.

- Designate a place in your home where you can pull away and be with God.
- Schedule time to be with the Lord. Yes; put it on your calendar if that helps!
- Keep your Bible, pens, notecards, commentaries, and any other tools you may need well-stocked and easily accessible at your reading place.
- Make a reading or study plan and ask someone to hold you accountable to it.
- If possible, make your space visible or someplace you see often. When you see it, be reminded that you meet with God there. Anticipate the next time you get to go to that place. But don't forget, you can meet with Him any place! This should help create a rhythm and reminder for you, but don't let it become a hurdle to spending time with Him in other places.
- Pray as you read, asking God to help you know Him and His Word better.
- Memorize Scripture and incorporate it into your prayers and daily speech.
- Know God's Word and live it out.

God's Word is living and active. Know it. Abide with Him in it. Be changed by it. Carry it to others and teach them to do the same.

Incorporating Other Spiritual Disciplines

As you cultivate patterns of prayer and Bible reading, you can also incorporate other spiritual disciplines. Be still, silent, and alone with God in secret. Get away for a more extended time and really practice Sabbath. Intentionally and regularly gather with other believers for prayer, worship, Bible reading, accountability, and fellowship. Serve others and serve alongside others.

Your patterns as a ministry leader may look different from the patterns of a person who serves differently, and this is okay; it just takes a bit of creativity and a lot of intentionality. For a season, I attended services with a church that met Saturday nights so I could be free to lead my church on Sunday mornings. This gave me time to regularly worship and to connect with other believers (who weren't asking me for new crayons or hand sanitizer), and it gave me the time and filled heart I needed to think clearly and make a plan for assimilating into my own church family.

Explore your options, seek counsel, and practice intentionality.

Be a Disciple Who Makes Disciples

Your role as a disciple-maker hinges on you being a growing and maturing disciple. Therefore, make it a priority to create time for your personal spiritual development. Ask other leaders in your church how they are growing. Commit to encourage and be encouraged by your brothers and sisters in these things and, together, cultivate spiritually healthy habits that you can pass on to one another and to the children you serve.

What about Growing My Leadership Skills?

by Bill Emeott

When I started in kids ministry back in the late 1980s, things looked very different than they do today. Computers and pagers were just making their way to the church; we were fortunate to have one of each to share between us all. Today, I carry a computer in my pocket and connect with friends halfway around the world as easily as those halfway down the hall. New discoveries, techniques, and methods are all around us, and we'd be wise to equip ourselves with those new skills for teaching biblical truths. We have to be learning and growing. We must be lifelong learners.

There are two reasons why people choose not to be lifelong learners: First, they think they're too busy; second, they think they know it all. Let's start with the know-it-all.

If you think you know it all, chances are, that's exactly who you are—a know-it-all—and you don't really know it all, at all. I've met a lot of leaders who think they've arrived. They've achieved a degree, have years of experience, and could write a book, so why would they work toward growing their leadership skills? This common trap can be the mistake that leaves you irrelevant and ineffective. Be careful. You can know a lot and still not know it all (no one does).

The second, which plagues us all, is a lack of time. I don't know anyone in kids ministry that would say they have time to spare. No one! Oftentimes we wake up in the morning with a list of "to-dos" that seems longer than the list we took to bed. I get it, I really do. But we need to make learning and growing a priority and a discipline and find the time to learn.

Like any discipline, it requires commitment and sometimes creativity. If you really don't have any more time in your day, ask yourself what you're doing with the time you have. How could you be more efficient so that growing your skills doesn't require quitting your job?

Consider these options for learning and growing your ministry skills:

Accredited Degree Programs. College and graduate school are more easily accessed today than ever before. Online education is a way of life. Consider the community colleges, Bible colleges, and seminaries that may offer opportunities for at-home learning. While receiving a degree is definitely rewarding, it might be an easier start to just enroll and start taking classes. One day you'll wake up and realize you're almost finished, but don't let the big picture intimidate your start.

Books. There are a plethora of leadership books. Kids ministry books are not as plentiful, but they are available. Ask around and get a few recommendations. Keep a book nearby for those times when you're waiting at the dentist office, or the tire dealer, or even when you just want to relax. A good book can become a trusted friend.

Webinars and Webcasts. There seems to be plenty of online training opportunities. My advice is to look carefully into where you spend your time, and oftentimes your money. It's easy for anyone to put anything out there. While I'm convinced that we can learn something from everyone, don't be misled by a flashy online program that may not offer credible counsel. Investigate and know what you're getting into.

Blogs. Everyone has a blog (or at least it seems that way). Ask a friend, surf the Web, and find a few blogs you trust and enjoy. Take five to ten minutes every day to read and learn.

Podcasts. Drive time for many of us can eat hours out of the week. What about using that time for learning? Download and listen to podcasts while driving and hear from successful ministry leaders. My drive time is about fifteen to twenty minutes one way, so I look for podcasts that fit that time frame or maybe double (half on the way to work and the other half on the way home).

Social Media. Opinions and training can be two very different things. However, there are several social media groups that offer support and information. Use discretion with these forums, but recognize them as excellent places to read about what others are doing and allow God to lead.

Peer Learning. Some of the best learning can take place from folks who are in the same boat as you. Look for peer groups. Consider starting one. Meet together regularly to share ideas and to consider things that have been tried and proven. Another benefit of friendships with peers in ministry is learning what not to do by listening to your friends' failures.

Mentors. If you're new in ministry, one of the best ways to learn and grow is to establish mentor relationships. Find a friend who's ahead of you in ministry and has seen the ropes and knows a little more than you do about getting across. Grow that friendship and allow that person to speak into your heart and ministry. Plan lunches or coffee breaks to discuss and learn.

A good friend of mine once said, "Be a student, not a critic." I've thought a lot about that over the years. It's easy to criticize and see the bad in something. Remember, hearing ideas that differ from yours exposes you to others' views and can also strengthen your opinions and beliefs. It's not what is said as much as where what's been said takes you.

Make the decision now to be a learner—a lifelong learner. Then turn around and be a teacher.

What about Boundaries?

by Bekah Stoneking

I often find myself saying "yes." I enjoy helping others, and I'm happy when people know they can rely on me. But in life, in leadership, and especially in children's ministry (with all its people and parts), saying "yes" too frequently can lead to feeling overwhelmed and fearing burnout.

Prayerfully setting boundaries, however, can help protect my well-being and fitness for ministry.

Remember Who You Are

Feeling like you're overextended can be daunting. But it can also be a blessing. It's in these stretched-too-thin moments that I most remember who I am—a finite creature made by an infinite, all-powerful, sovereign God.

I pray you allow this reminder to be freeing to you. You don't hold the world in your hands—God does! Your ministry and your church belong to Him. Let this be at

> Your ministry and your church belong to Him.

the forefront of your mind as you make decisions about ministry and boundaries.

It's in your moments of finiteness where you can point people to God's "otherness." He is steady and all-powerful. Be transparent about your human limits and take them as reminders to rely on God.

Take Care of Yourself

In 1 Corinthians, Paul urges the believers to imitate him as he imitates Christ. As a ministry leader, your chief role is that of a disciple who is making other disciples. This means that your relationship with Jesus is your primary task. Whether you're making disciples at home or at church, it is your responsibility is to be maturing in your faith. Secure whatever people or resources you need to support your spiritual development.

You should also care for yourself physically. God created your body to need certain things to function properly.

Build healthy patterns into your life like:

- Regular, consistent time with the Lord in Bible study and prayer
- Regular fellowship with other believers
- Accountability
- Good sleeping habits
- Sabbath
- Proper nutrition
- Physical exercise
- Fun!

Take a walk, play a musical instrument, visit a new coffee shop, or work with your hands. Honor God by making time to enjoy the good things He has given. Setting boundaries that allow you to care for the body God has given you and to grow in your relationship with Jesus will help your disciple-making and ministry efforts flourish.

Prioritize Your Family

Ministering to Your Spouse and Children

If you are married or if you have children, these people are your first ministry. God has called you to these people. Bear this in mind and steward these gifts.

Minister to your family by:

- Placing your family's activities and needs on your calendar
- Protecting your family's schedule as you'd protect other appointments
- Seeking accountability for how you balance family, ministry, and work
- Encouraging your co-laborers to honor their families on their calendars
- Verbally and publicly supporting your fellow leaders as they minister to their families
- Holding your calendar with an open hand

Knowing when to say "no" to a good thing so you can say "yes" to a great thing and knowing when to change your calendar to accommodate an urgent need will help you become schedule savvy.

Caring for Yourself as a Single Leader

The apostle Paul esteems unmarried believers for their freedom to more fully focus on God. If you are single, you may (rightly!) feel led to give generously of your time.

But you should also be wise with your time.

Being single means not having a partner to help take care of things at home. It also means not having the accountability of someone who sees as deeply into your life as a spouse might. Steward the good portion God has given you by intentionally scheduling time to care for your home, your neighbors, and yourself, and by allowing other believers to hold you accountable for how you balance self-care, spiritual growth, ministry, and life.

Embrace the Grace

Wherever you find yourself—whether in a season of sprinting or limping—remember who you are and remember Who made you. He sees you and He has everything you need.

The Bible teaches that God is rich in mercy and that He lavishes His grace upon His people. Indeed, God has dealt graciously with you. Embrace His grace, apply that grace to yourself, and be quick to extend grace to others as you grow in Christ and as you serve His church together.

What about a Support System?

by Bill Emeott

By design, we do ministry better with others. Acts 2:42 tells us that the early church "devoted themselves to the apostles' teaching, to *fellowship*, to the breaking of bread, and to prayer." God has wired us, at least at some level, to fellowship and support each other. Kids ministry is not the exception, and this could very well make the difference for a healthy and successful ministry.

Everybody needs somebody, and that holds true in kids ministry. We need family, friends, and ministry colleagues to complement us and surround us with love and support.

Family

The only relationship more important than family is your relationship with God, but too many ministers have allowed their ministry to overshadow the importance of family. Don't hear me wrong. If you have accepted the position of kids ministry leader, and particularly if you're getting paid to do that job, you need to honor that commitment and give that work 100 percent, but you won't be successful if you don't also—more so than your work—honor your family.

> The only relationship more important than family is your relationship with God.

Most ministers I know are workaholics putting in endless hours and sacrificing family (and self) to get the job done. I understand that mentality (I struggle here too), but we need to understand that prolonged seasons of fifty- to sixty-hour workweeks are not healthy and will eventually catch up with you and your relationship with your family.

There will be seasons when you spend countless hours preparing and executing ministry. There will be times when you are called away from a scheduled family event because of an emergency or a crisis. Find opportunities to repay that time away and to remind your family of their importance and of your appreciation for their support. Don't forget that for you, your family is the most important family in your ministry.

Your family should be one of your greatest support systems. Home should be a respite and a place that you can go to recharge and regroup from the business of kids ministry. Be careful (and intentional) to not lose that haven because you've consistently failed to give priority to your family.

Friends

Ministry can be very lonely. Be intentional about making and maintaining friendships. Prayer partners, ministry team members, and other staff members need to become a part of your ministry, but they can also make for great lifelong friends. Take the time to share life (not just church life). Share about your family; share your hobbies and mutual interests. Find opportunities to talk about things not related to ministry. Cultivate good friendships.

Every minister needs a friend who doesn't have the same pastor as he does. That's right, you heard me correctly. You need to develop friends who don't go to your church. You need a friend who you can talk (not gossip, but speak openly and honestly) with about church issues without it affecting their worship on Sunday.

It's important to talk about things without burdening the listener. While spouses make great "best" friends (and they should be), be careful how much you share and consider how it will affect them. If you are struggling with a fellow staff member or church leader, it could really hinder your spouse's relationship with that person and might even hinder their ability to attend, support, and be the church member they've been called to be. Cultivate a trusted friend outside your church's fellowship.

Colleagues

Seek out a group of like-minded kids ministry leaders. You may have to organize such a group, but the benefits are worth the effort. This group will regularly gather to share ideas, learn about trends, and support each other in ministry. This can be an organized group with a scheduled agenda, a casual group of friends who meet for fellowship and support, or better yet, a combination of both.

Consider finding a mentor. This colleague in ministry will have been where you now are, weathered many storms in ministry, and is willing to share from their experiences and give their opinion and solicited advice. This mentor most likely will be a season or two ahead of you in life/ministry and can objectively give perspective based on her journey.

One of the joys in ministry is to return the investment that others made in you. If you're reading this and are in the second half of your ministry journey, consider seeking out a younger minister in whom to invest and mentor. They're out there, but may not know the value of a Paul/Timothy relationship, or may be afraid to ask.

God knows our need for a support system and has already prepared one for you. Seek Him, seek them, and together enjoy life and ministry together.

What about Burnout?

by Bill Emeott

"I'm so busy taking care of everybody else, I'm falling apart!"

These are the words recently shared with me by a close kids ministry friend. As she shared her struggles, tears began to stream down her face, and I could tell she was close to throwing in the towel and stepping away from her ministry. Tired, frustrated, and hurting, she was on the verge of burnout.

A clinical definition of burnout is: a state of emotional, mental, and physical exhaustion caused by excessive and prolonged stress. As stress continues, you begin to lose the interest or motivation that led you to take on your role in the first place.

Burnout can cause one to feel a loss of interest, motivation, and energy. It reduces productivity and gives a sense of helplessness and hopelessness. People suffering from burnout can be cynical, resentful, and empty.

Ever feel that way?

Most of us have bad days. We get bored, overloaded, or feel unappreciated. When the dozens of balls we keep in the air aren't noticed, let alone rewarded, we can quickly become frustrated and consider giving up. However, if you're feeling that way *most* of the time, you might be flirting with burnout.

Some common risk factors for burnout include your personality type, what you bring with you, your health, and your relationship with Christ. Other external factors might include pressures of expectations to exceed, unclear expectations, conflicts with others and others' values, a mismatch of job skills, no freedom to dream and be who you believe God has created you to be, and consistently living in the urgent.

I think the majority of kids ministry leaders are bent toward hard work, giving much, and neglecting themselves in the process. Remember John 10:10: "A thief comes only to steal and kill and destroy." Satan would like nothing more than to destroy your ministry through prolonged stress and eventual burnout. But the promise of John 10:10 comes in the second half, "I have come so that they may have life and have it in abundance."

Ministry certainly implies a responsibility to care for and minister to people. The old adage, "They don't care how much you know until they know how much you care," stands true. But how can we prevent burnout?

We have to take care of ourselves! It's just that simple. Here are five areas to consider:

1. **Take care of yourself spiritually:** Your greatest asset in ministry isn't your talents, your skills, or your resource room. Your greatest asset is your relationship

with God. Do not neglect your time with Him. Refresh your spiritual disciplines. Find time for reading and studying the Scriptures. Talk with God (not just to Him). Worship regularly. These things make a difference. Don't be so busy serving Him that you don't take the time to be with Him.

2. **Take care of yourself physically:** The Bible teaches that our body is the temple in which the Holy Spirit dwells. Some of us need to clean up the temple and consider our physical health. If you don't take care of your physical body, eventually you'll "reap what you have sown" and you'll be on your back. Those extra pounds; that lack of sleep; those drive-through meals can really take a toll on your ministry. Find time to relax and get away from work.

3. **Take care of yourself mentally:** Intentionally restructure your poor habits. Be a forever student. Keep your mind sharp and your ministry fresh by reading, listening, and learning. If you think you know it all, you're wrong, and you'll struggle.

4. **Take care of yourself socially:** When's the last time you socialized with adults apart from your ministry? Cultivate friendships that don't focus around your ministry. Talk about the weather, sports, your favorite TV show. Spend time with family and friends laughing and sharing life. Join a support/prayer group if necessary, or start one with friends you know who are struggling too.

5. **Take care of yourself emotionally:** Too many times we bottle our feelings, let life "shake us up," and then explode all over the place, oftentimes making rash judgments with harsh consequences. Learn to manage

your stress and saddle your emotions. Take a deep breath, take a walk around the block (apply point two here), talk with a friend . . . but don't let your emotions get the best of you. Remember Proverbs 15:1: "A gentle answer turns away anger, but a harsh word stirs up wrath."

Ours is *abundant life* . . . it already exists! You don't have to create it, repair it, beg for it, try to figure it out, cry over it, or figure out how to fund it. You don't even have to talk someone into it! It is complete in the cross. Know that you belong to a Savior who wants nothing more for you than to live a fully abundant life in Him!

> Your greatest asset is your relationship with God.

NOTES

1. Taken from the Bible Skills for Kids poster; https://www.lifeway.com/en/product-family/bible-skills-for-kids.

2. The kids ministry expression of this mission statement could be something like this: Our kids ministry exists to glorify God by introducing children and families to Jesus and leading them to follow Christ (http://fbcgoodlettsville.com/).

3. Note that none of the below are exhaustive, but should rather serve as a starting point. Make sure to conduct additional research, as noted in the third bullet point above.

4. The stats came from the most recent Annual Church Profile (SBC).

5. Ibid.

6. Curriculum Evaluation Worksheet

7. https://factsandtrends.net/2017/09/29/10-traits-of-generation-z/

8. http://thomrainer.com/2017/05/five-reasons-church-members-attend-church-less-frequently/

9. For more about learning preferences, see the following books that stem from the theory of multiple intelligences by Howard Gardner, https://www.amazon.com/default/e/B000APAQWW/ref=sr_ntt_srch_lnk_1?qid=1531681817&sr=8-1&redirectedFromKindleDbs=true.

10. See https://www.lifeway.com/en/product-family/bible-skills-for-kids.

11. http://thomrainer.com/2017/05/five-reasons-church-members-attend-church-less-frequently/

12. Jana Magruder and LifeWay Research, *Nothing Less: Engaging Kids in a Lifetime of Faith* (Nashville: LifeWay, 2016).

13. *New Oxford American Dictionary*

14. Tony Reinke, *12 Ways Your Phone Is Changing You* (Wheaton, IL: Crossway, 2017), 60.

15. https://www.desiringgod.org/messages/prayer-the-work-of-missions

16. https://www.christianity.com/christian-life/prayer/prayer-as-breathing -11554942.html